I0471069

Sulat ng Kaluluwa

Writing of the Soul

Art of Kristian Kabuay
Voices of the Filipino Diaspora

www.Baybayin.com

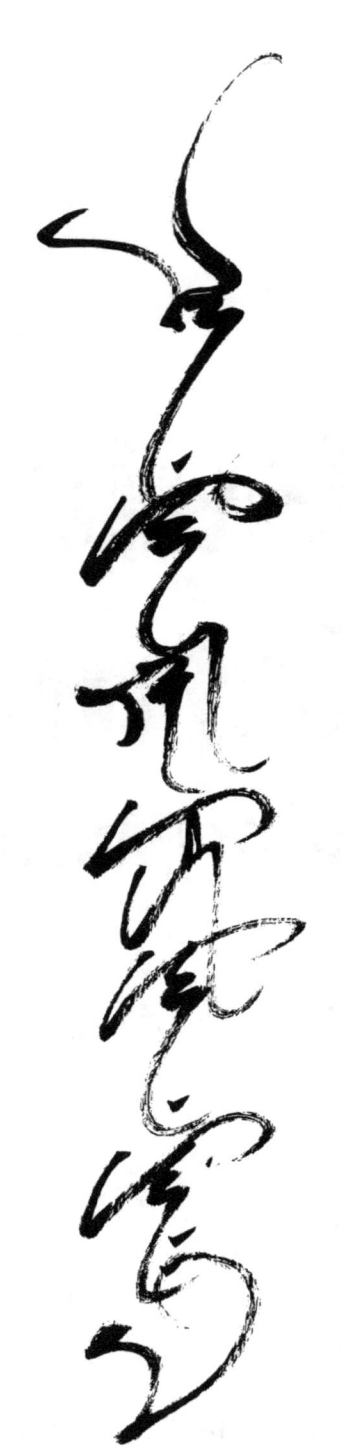

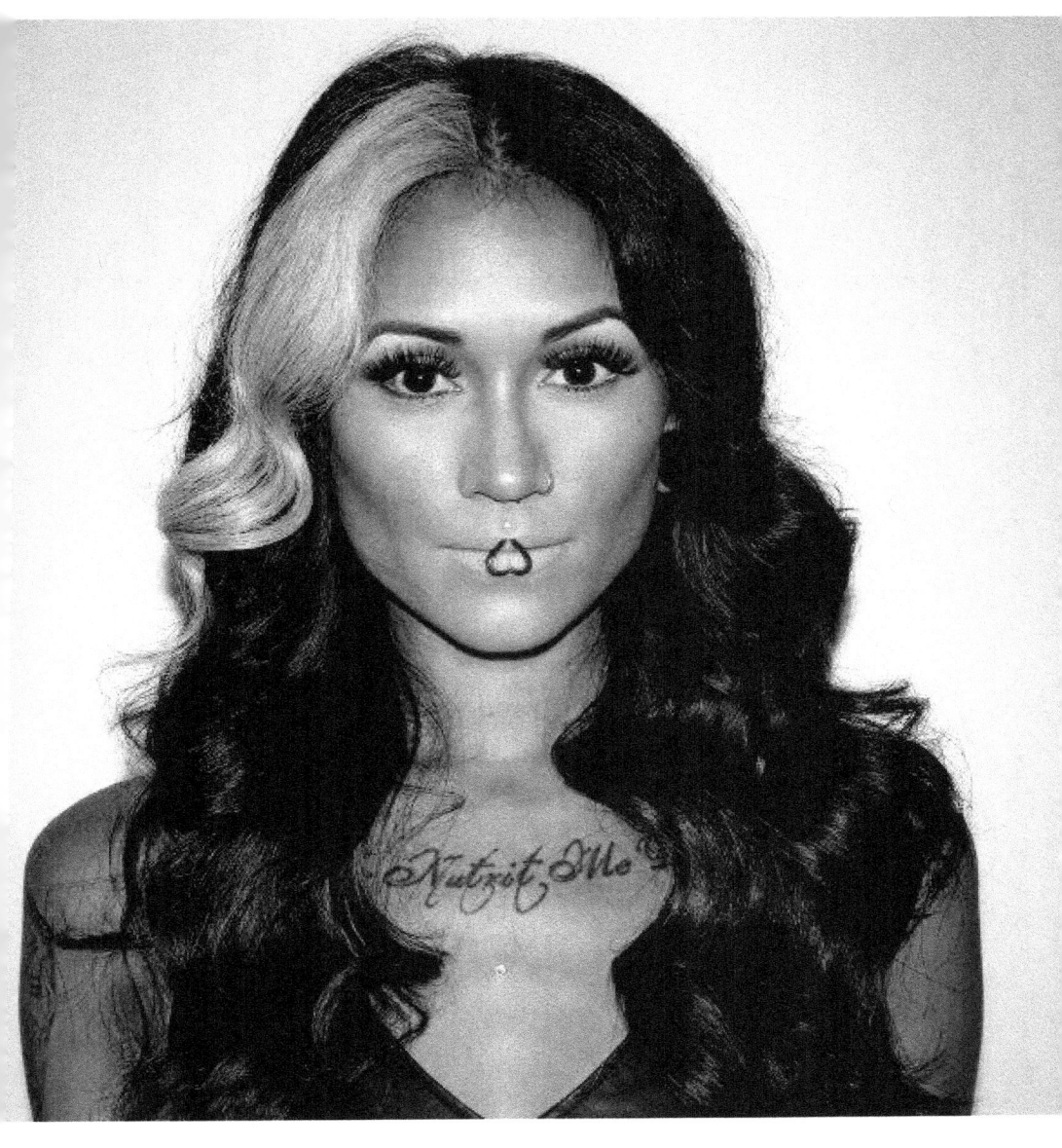

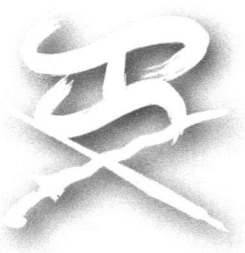

Cover model: Chloe Rainwater
Cover photography: Kristian Kabuay
Editorial consultant: Mitzi Duque Ruiz

Published by Kristian Kabuay
Contact info@baybayin.com or 925-396-5969 for any inquiries

Available for workshops, speaking and art shows world wide

Connections
Sulatngkaluluwa.com
Baybayin.com
Kabuay.com
Facebook.com/Baybayin
Facebook.com/SulatngKaluluwa
Twitter.com/Baybayin
Instagram.com/Baybayin

Contents

Salamat - Thank you

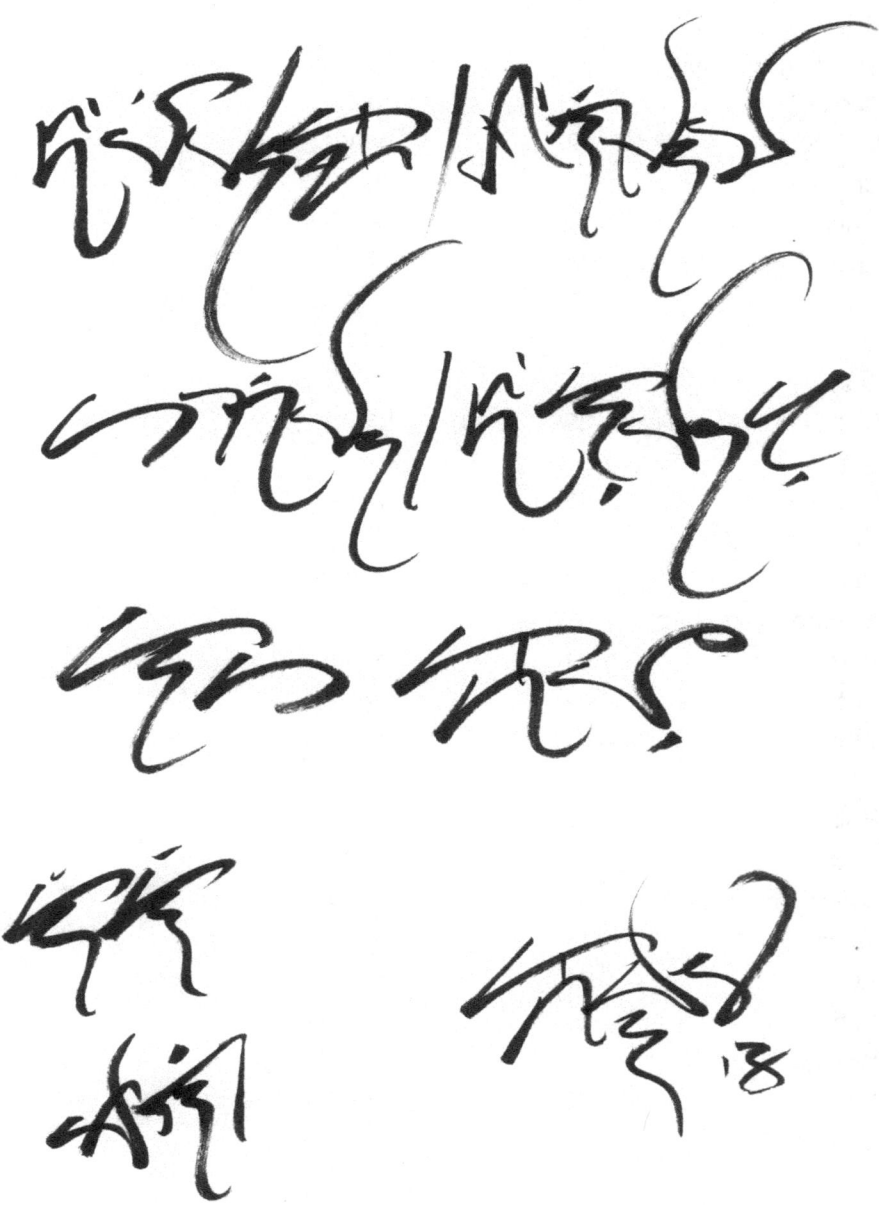

Acknowledgements

These are in no particular order....right off the top of the head :)

Philippine Consul General of San Francisco
Philippine Embassy of Paris, France
Philippine Embassy of London, UK
Philippine Embassy of Madrid, Spain
Philippine Embassy of Brussels, Belgium
Center for Babaylan Studies
Asian Art Museum
Bayanihan Center
Manila Heritage Foundation
Power ng Pinoy
Philippine Generations
Baybayin Buhayin
P&P Tattoos
Dream Jungle Tattoo
San Francisco Public Library
Oakland Asian Cultural Center
FPAC
FAAE
PAWA
YFPA
WIPCaps
BayaniArt
PST Gear
Sari-Sari Underground
Filipino Brand
TeamManila
Archepeligo Books
Philippine Expressions
Reflections of Asia
Baybayin Buhayin
UST Archives

Simula - Beginning

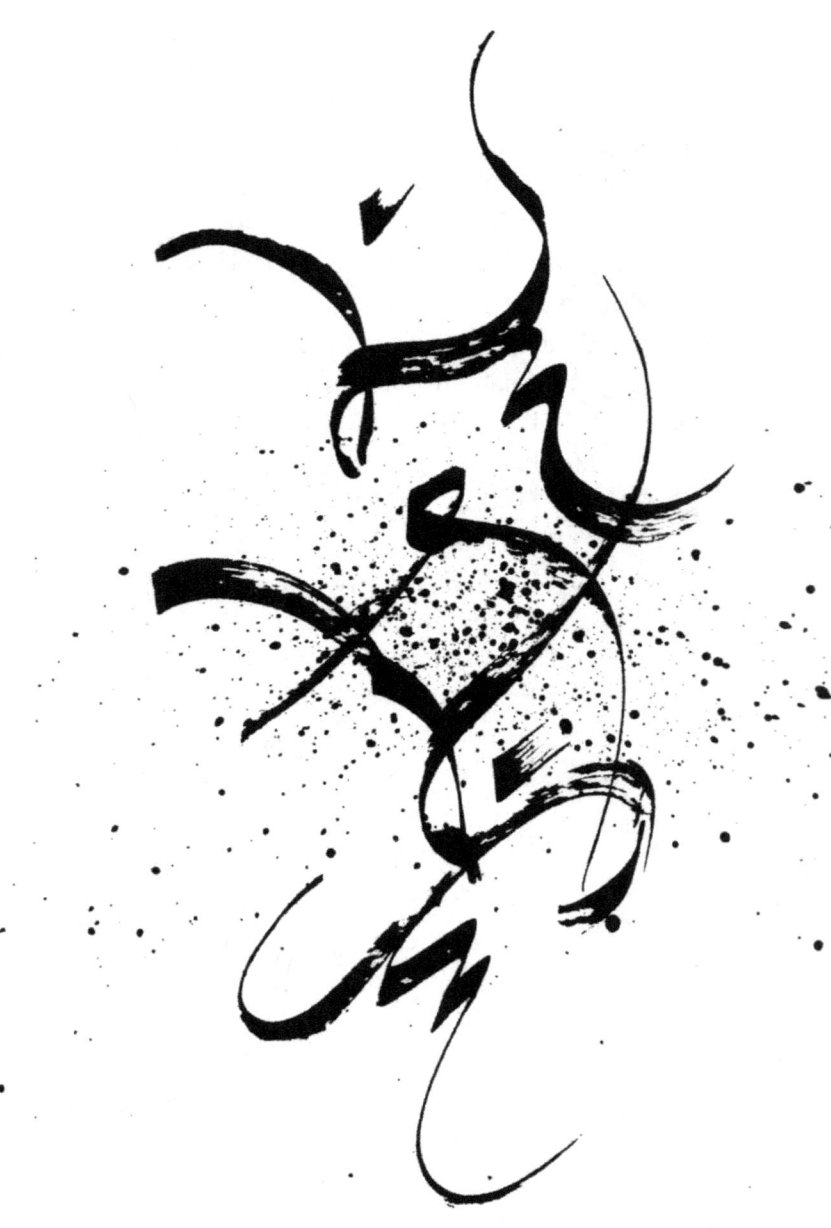

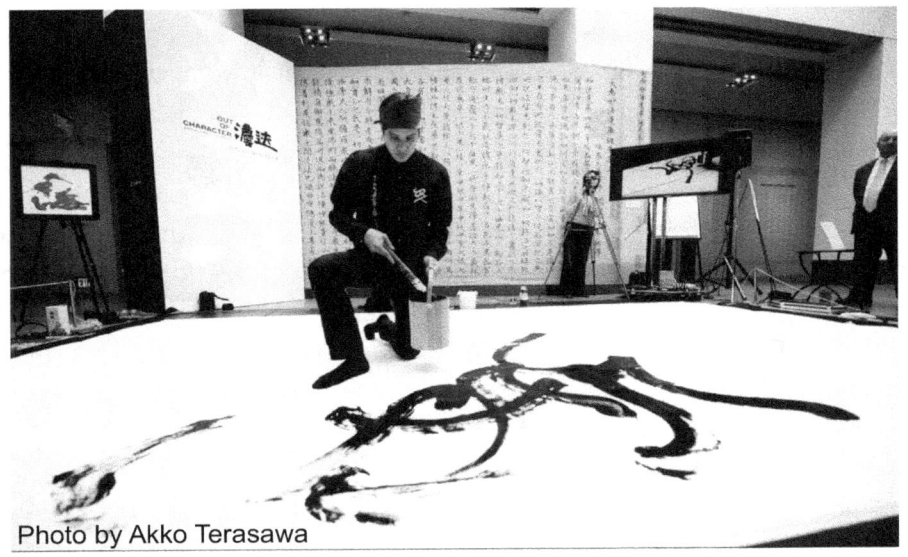

Photo by Akko Terasawa

I remember being moved by Kristian's landscape photo on his Facebook page - physically and spiritually moved to action. I could feel my ancestors and a true call to move forward. I had been stagnant and confused, doubting who I am, why I'm here, and the purpose in my life. I'd had glimpses of inspiration since childhood. Something from his symbolism and the energy he brought forth gave me confidence and reassurance. Kristian has a peaceful and silent way about him that's grounding, and he's been an amazing brother. I look to him for inspiration and no-nonsense feedback. He's sincere in his delivery and actions. He gifted me with a version of simula that symbolically used two brushes and looked a bit "messy" compared to his larger image that drew me. Perfect, as I was merging my masculine and feminine elements to take action in my life, yet staying true to my tender and heart centered purpose. It's important to me to balance and honor both my male and female elements.

I think of the moment of creation, the acknowledgment of our spark within, what it takes to go from possible and probable to happening now and how we choose. Sometimes we're just moved, like when I found Kristian's photo and knew I had to contact him. My life and my daughter's life and everyone I know and serve are gifted from my taking action and trusting my instinct. I have wondered in the past, what makes the difference? How do I know? Through self-observation we learn our patterns, our values and what truly moves us to action; consistent action then at times an end.

The sweetness of a new beginning, the discipline of beginning again and starting from scratch with new possibilities, even if toward the same goals we've pursued for a lifetime or lifetimes... all represented in the symbolism and script Kristian created.

I felt the image that first called me was calling us all -- all workers of the light leading with heart, all from our indigenous heritage -- forward, to come together. I feel Kristian is a way show-er, a warrior bridging both dark and light, past and present. His art is rich in heritage and presence. As an energy worker and healer, I was fascinated by the power that comes through his art, and even more streaming through from our ancestors.

Simula is a statement from within, a choosing to actively participate, as well as an acknowledgement that it's time, your time, take action. I'm proud of our heritage, my roots, all that comes together through and for me and for our generation. I'm honored to walk with Kristian in honoring who we've been while staying in the present and being practical about where we're going and what we're creating. I still remember him sharing how it upsets him to see and know so many who have potential they haven't used. Therefore—simula -- start... with whatever you've got right now, even if you feel insecure, even if you feel you're not ready. When your internal gun shot, start button, is pressed, go for it and know you'll be supported. Take action. Like they say, leap and the net will appear.

Everything merges into a place of power here and now, as we choose to begin. Action, dreams unfolding, utilizing all your resources, having a clear direction, trusting your right action... all of these elements and more come together when you finally say and choose now... I begin. My ancestors have been and still are; everything is happening around me, and my unique contribution, my conscious choice is this. I may as well be proud and contribute the best I can.

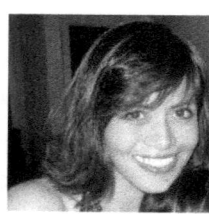

Jasmine Therese Esguerra
San Francisco, California, USA
Purewellnessintl.com

17 Base Characters

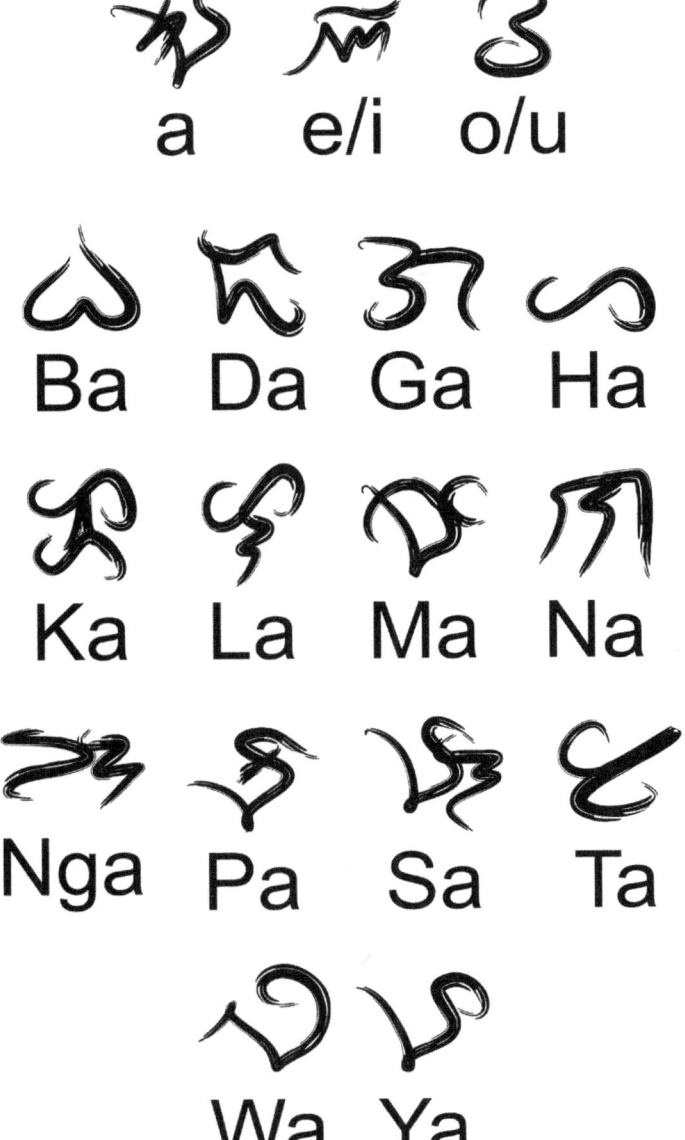

a   e/i   o/u

Ba   Da   Ga   Ha

Ka   La   Ma   Na

Nga   Pa   Sa   Ta

Wa   Ya

Introduction

Baybayin is the writing system used in the so-called Philippines prior to Spanish colonization. I 1st came into contact with the script in 1993 when saw a photo of the Katipunan, a Philippine revolutionary society who fought for independence from Spain. I was intrigued with the revolutionaries and talked to an old man about the Katipunan at a Filipino Festival at the Bill Graham Civic Auditorium in San Francisco. I asked him about what I thought was a capital "I" standing for Independence, on the flag. I remember how blown away I was to learn that it was our very own indigenous writing system. From then on, Baybayin became my obsession.

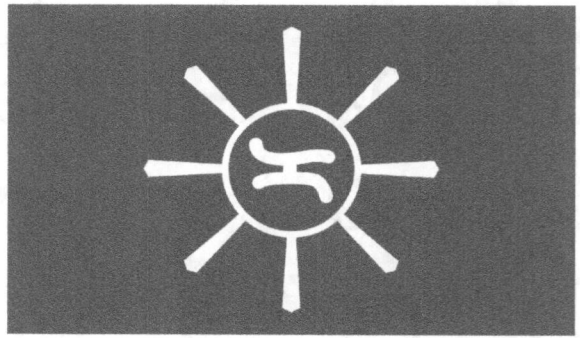

Sulat ng Kaluluwa (Writing of the soul) are the stories of my clients, people I've met and complete strangers through the years promoting Filipino identity through Baybayin. These stories range from the heartbreaking to inspiring to funny. While I say "Voices of the Filipino Diaspora", I challenge the traditional meaning of diaspora of "The movement, migration, or scattering of a people away from an established or ancestral homeland" as defined by Merriam-Webster. Can you be part of the Filipino diaspora if you live in the Philippines or go back after many years abroad? What if you have no Filipino blood at all but have a connection to the Philippines and the culture? To me, the diaspora is more of a state of mind. It transcends physical migration to another land. In the Philippines, you have kids growing up learning English as their 1st language. You have Kapampangan kids learning Tagalog instead of their native language. With globalization, we have the world within arms reach but sometimes forget what we already have.

In 2010, I was preparing a book about Filipino tattoos and their stories based on my PinoyTattoos.com website but ultimately decided that I didn't want my art to only be associated with tattoos. I felt that this project was better left for a tattoo artist to take on. About a year ago, I started to think about a much needed update to my 1st book, An Introduction to Baybayin I put out in 2009 but got distracted with other projects. I like the concept of the Filipino Tattoos project but would use Baybayin instead. While I had over 100 stories from commissions, I wanted to start fresh with the context of putting out a book of community stories. They gave me a word or name and told me the story behind it and I would create the art. The initial idea was to have submissions handwritten but it's pretty rare for people to hand-write letters.

Each piece featured in this book was all hand written in over the Labor Day long weekend from August 30 to September 2, 2013. I started on some pieces as early as January 2013 but scrapped them because I wanted to use the same batch of ink for a unified look. My work explores Filipino culture in the diaspora. Using Baybayin, as a foundation, I incorporate and deconstruct calligraphy and graffiti methods. My pieces can be described as didactic art that is meant both to entertain and to instruct. Themes explored are identity, poverty, death, love and duality.

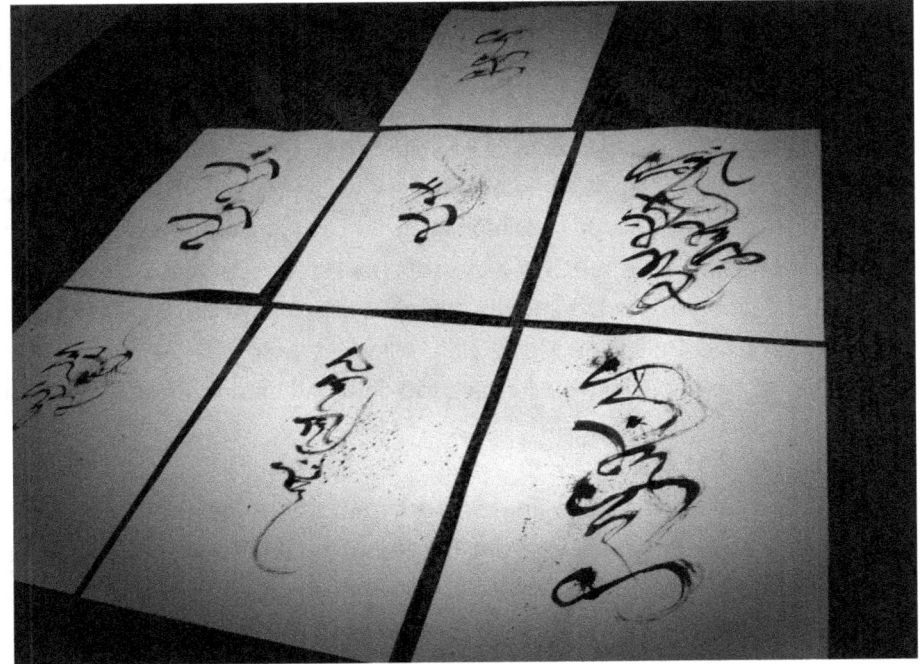

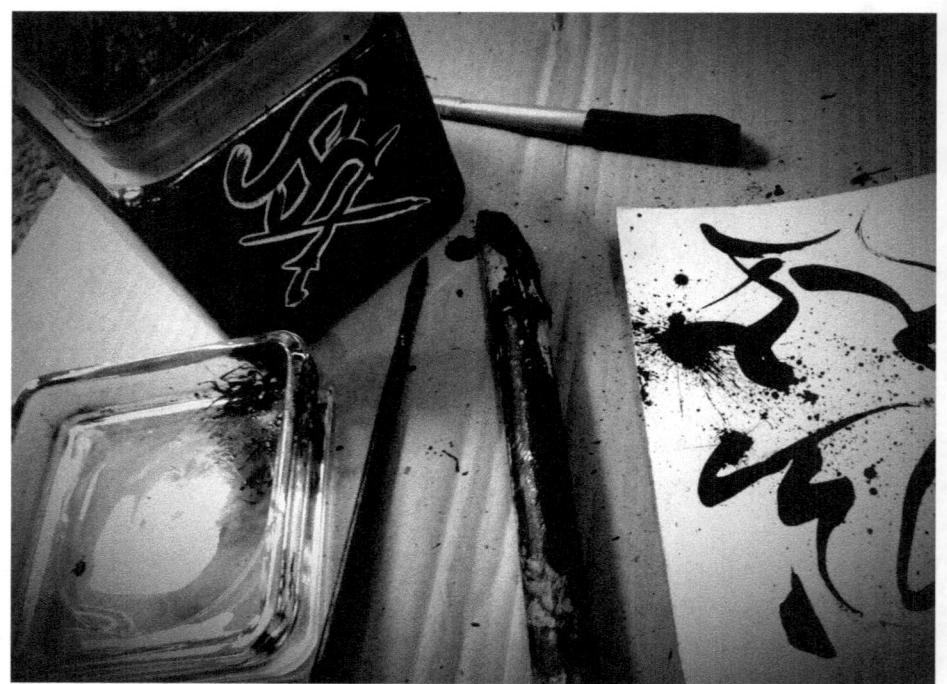

One of my favorite stories in this book is from Mari from San Francisco, who carries the middle name of Rosario passed down from her grandmother. This story is from their ancestral homeland of Nasugbu, Batangas, Philippines. She wrote about the Burning of Lumang Simbahan (Old Church) where hundreds of men, women and children of Nasugbu were gathered and killed by Spanish troops who set the Lumang Simbahan on fire in 1896. In his Batangas y Su Provincia, Manuel Sastron, a Spanish historian, briefly described the church as he saw it in 1895, a year before it was destroyed. Sastron wrote that the church, which was then 43 years old, was well-attended to by the zealous parish priest, Don Leocadio Dimanlig, who was intimately called by the townspeople as Padre Kadio. He served as parish priest of Nasugbu from 1895 to 1900 and was destined to see his church and the town destroyed during the first phase of the Philippine Revolution. Pilgrims, many of them from distant provinces, come especially on Fridays to light candles and pray in the church ruins.

Ayvee is a talented rapper/singer/model from Los Angeles, California, who submitted a story in lyrical for from her song "Aircon Rich". It brought back memories of my years living in Manila. The general idea was that if you had aircon, you were "rich" and the colder the aircon or the ability to leave it on 24-7, gave you more clout.

The funniest story in this book is courtesy of Tiffany from San Francisco, Californial, who tells the story about her mom and the Filipino slang term for vagina.

There were a few surprises but the one that stands out as the most random is from Magdalena of Poland. I 1st came into contact with her when she sent a Facebook message to my PinoyTattoos page inquiring about a tattoo of my Baybayin artwork. She wanted to know what the artwork meant and a little history about the script. After consulting with her for about a week, I realized that she wasn't even Filipino. I assumed that she was the usual mestiza (1/2 white) you find in Europe. Even her name sounds Pinoy (Slang term for Filipinos).

Closing out the book is Iraya. She poetically tells her story about her experience growing up in San Francisco, California. from personal exploration of being mestiza, I-Hotel, multiculturalism and coming of age. Her story will bring back memories to any Filipino growing up in San Francisco roaming the streets of SOMA in the 70's & 80's.

Each one of these personal stories are also your stories. Pass them to your loved ones to keep our tradition of story telling alive. I hope this book inspires you to create something to keep the legacy of YOU alive. As more and more Filipinos settle all over the world, it's important that we keep parts of our culture where ever we end up to pass on to the next generation. What have you learned that you can pass on to your family, kids or community? Have you learned cooking from your lola? What about language? Martial arts? Dancing? In the information age, there's no excuse. Thank you to all the storytellers in this book.

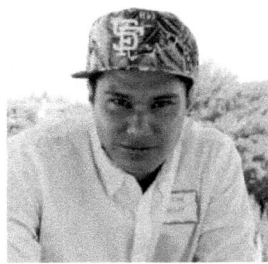

Kristian Kabuay
San Francisco, California, USA
9/16/2013

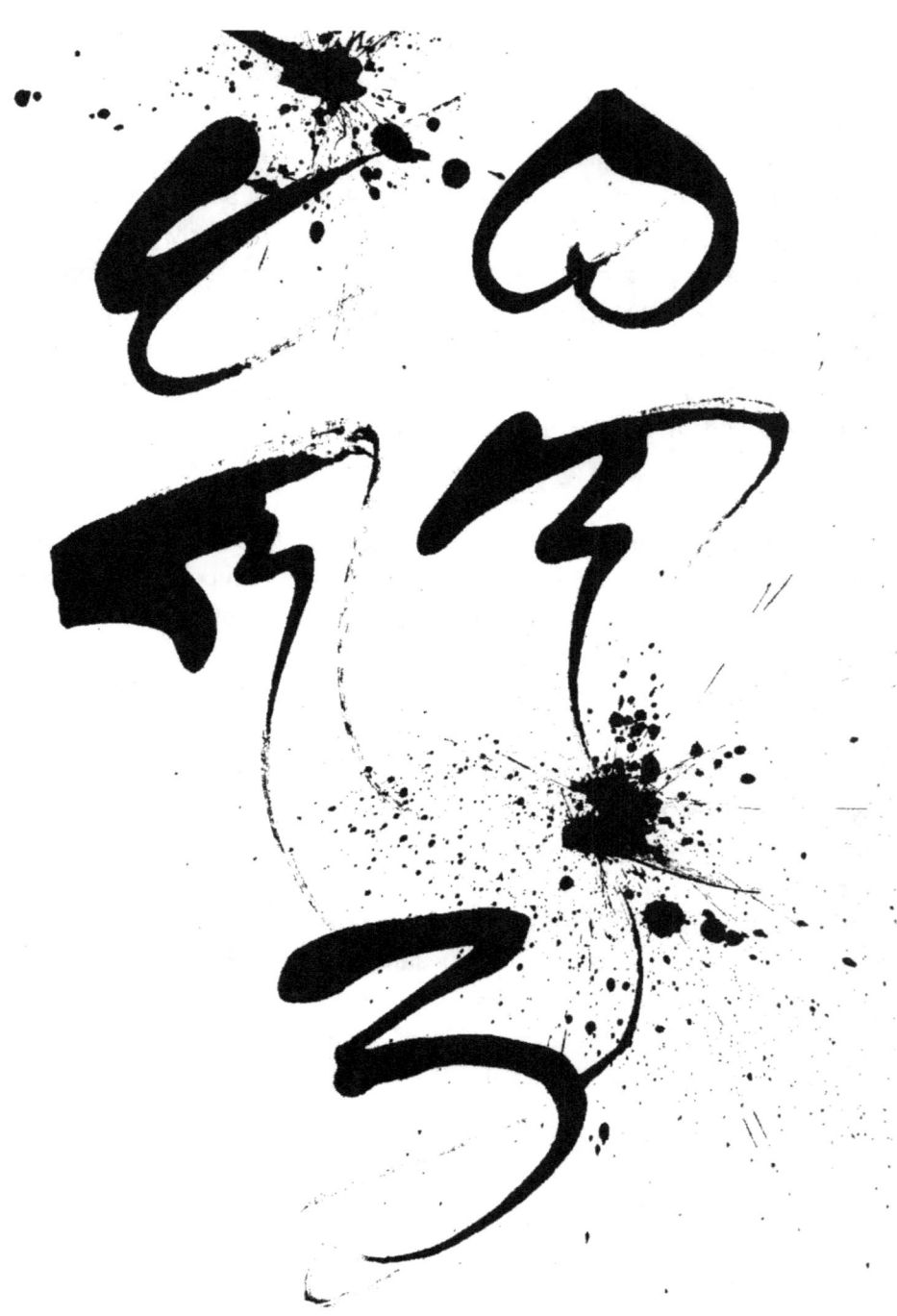

Tibay ng Loob - Resilience

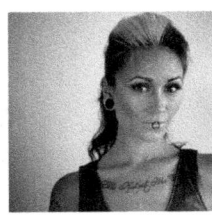

Chloe
Oakland, California, USA
FB: SFUMATObyChloe

Living between two different households until I was 16 years old; being kicked out of my mom's house when I was 13 years old; living on my own at the age of 16; experiencing heartbreak--the kind that deprives one of sleep, appetite, joy, and that sends shock-waves of wrenching pain, causing something so intangible to feel so physical--that kind of heartbreak, twice in my life; battling a variety of eating disorders; battling feelings of displacement and loneliness due to constantly moving; finding acceptance and identity as a Mestiza; finding acceptance and identity as a lesbian; saying "goodbye" to friends and family stolen away by Cancer--these perils, along with others unlisted (I have to create some mystery) undeniably formed or rather deformed, me into the woman I am today. Who I am today, however, is more importantly the molding and result of how I have persevered through life's challenges. I am able to share this short story about myself because I never gave up in life, I never "threw in the towel" or waved the white flag of surrender. I buckled to my knees multiple times when my strength and faith were fleeting, and I contemplated suicide on more than one occasion, but I have risen and I am alive; that is why I am the woman I am today, and why the word "resilience" speaks volumes to me.

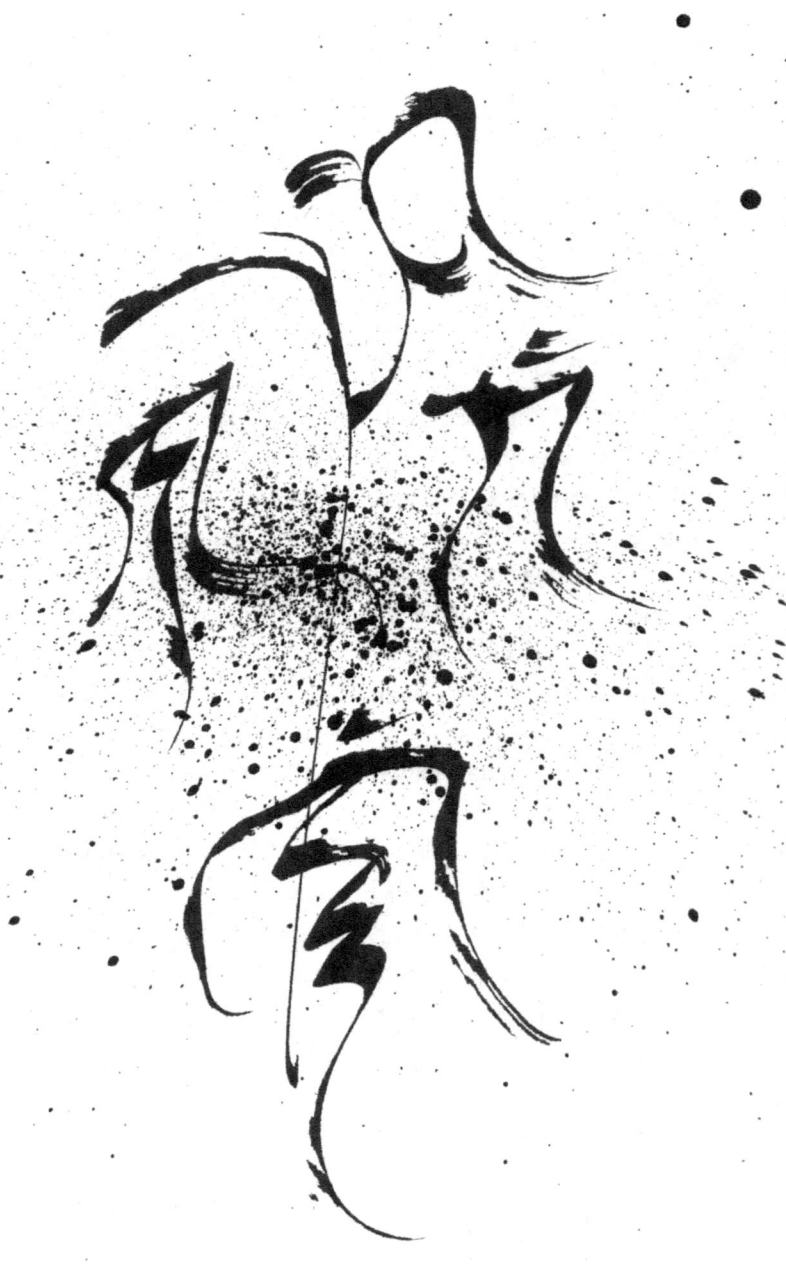

Panaginip - Dream

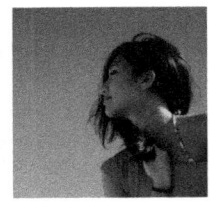

Marinel
Milan, Italy

I am a dreamer. I dream of things I have yet to see, of faraway places, of absolute freedom, of true love. I am content and comfortable in my small world, of this busy and lively metropolis I live in, of the caring people surrounding me; nevertheless, I dream of bigger and better things. I dream to fly away one day, travel around the world, free to go wherever I want to go, connect with people of diverse cultures, and find the man who will steal my heart.

I am a daydreamer. I visualise stories everywhere, I construct new realities, I imagine alternative endings. I make plans for the future and hope for them to come true. I find myself staring at the sky sometimes, and in my head thoughts mix up with fantasies: I build castles in the air.

I am an escapist. I run away from the unpleasant things in my life with my mind, with my imagination. Sometimes I go into denial... I avoid facing responsibilities and life problems by dreaming a different present, a better future. I refuse to accept one reality, thus I create my own versions of it.

I am an idealist. I dream of an ideal world; a world where nature prevails over concrete, where money and power don't create wars, where everyone is accepted for who they are, no matter what. However, trains would still run late, we would still be at the mercy of the weather, and the universe would still be a mystery for mankind. Perfection is not essential in this ideal world of mine.

Truth is, I am a hopeless visionary. I live in my own bubble, and sometimes I get lost in my own illusions. I am the 'what if' kind of girl. What if things were just a little bit different? What if I had done this instead of that? What if I had been to this place instead of that other one? The endless possibilities of what could have been give me dizzy spells; and when I resurface to the real world, I always feel a little bit sad and disappointed.

This is me, a perpetual dreamer.

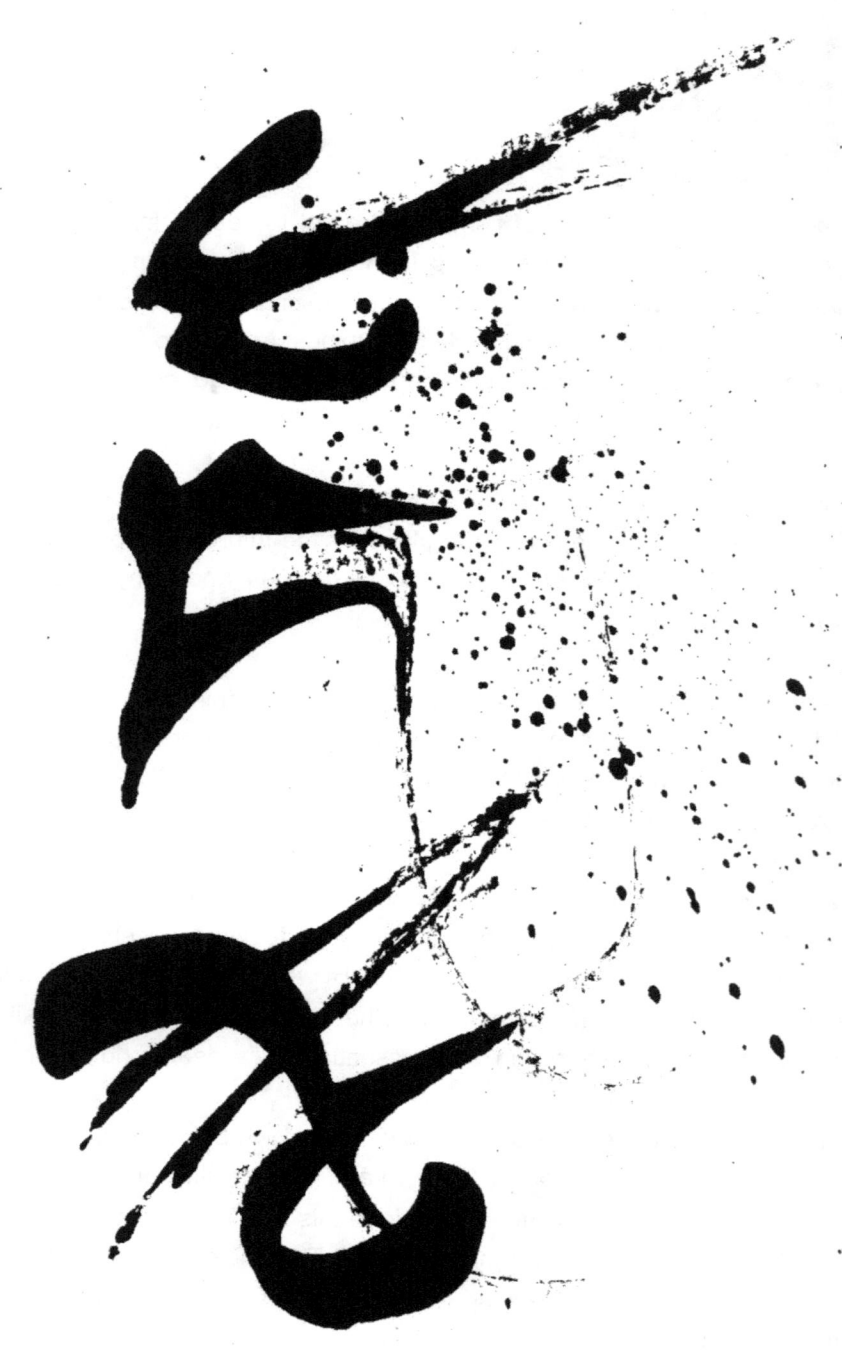

Tandaan - Remember

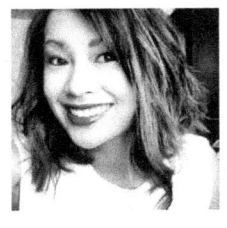

Arwin
Dublin, California, USA

When I was seven years old, I left the Philippines for the first time and "forever". My mom, my younger sister, and I were finally moving to the States to join my Dad who had been working and living there for a year. For the past four years before that, I only saw my Dad every six months for two weeks at a time. He had a common story: Overseas Filipino Worker in Saudi Arabia, trying to get his foot in the door as an engineer at Ericsson. Getting a transfer to the U.S. was the ultimate goal and after years of sacrificing and watching his family grow from afar, we were finally able to reunite in the "promised land".

I remember the night we left. My grandmother, my sister, and I were sitting on a bench at the tindahan across the street. She was crying, she was kissing our faces, she was saying goodbye because she would not be coming to the airport with us. She said "Laging mo tandaan kung saan ka galing. Huwag mo akong kalimutan. Mahal na mahal kita," Always remember where you came from. Don't forget me. I love you so much.

I remember, Nanay. I remember my language, I remember my culture, I remember my family. I never forgot where I came from and how it has shaped who I am today. Her parting words have instilled in me the importance of retaining an awareness of ones heritage in this increasingly globalized world. My beloved Nanay passed away in February 2010, but I honor her by remembering. In my thoughts, in my values, and in the daily presentation of my being, I always remember you and where I came from.

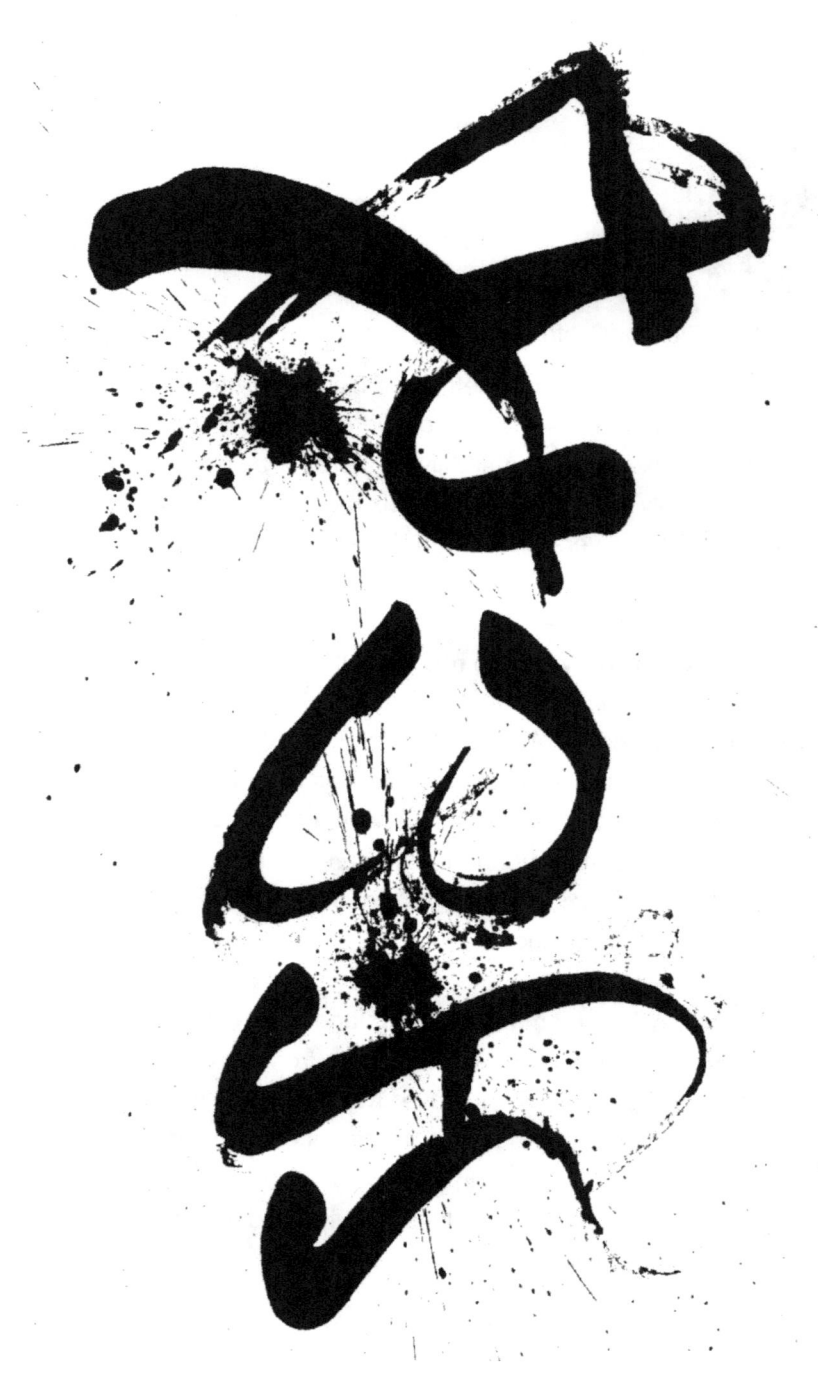

Mumbaki - Healer

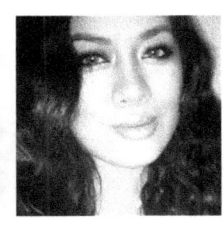

Luzviminda
Seattle, Washington, USA

"Home is where the heart is."

But when your heart is split in two places, how do you piece your home and your heart back together again? The Philippines is this geographical location that as a young girl I was taught to point to on a globe. Pointing to this place that differentiated me from the other kids, who didn't even know where they came from on the other side of the globe, on this continent called Europe which they didn't seem to have any particular feelings for. They went home with homework assignments to ask their parents where they came from because they did not come from Alabama, Alaska, Arizona, Arkansas, Colorado, Connecticut...I was not assigned homework. I could point to this far away land of islands that were thousands of miles away. So many miles that my mind could not compute the distance because I was still so young that I hadn't even learned that number yet. Not only did I know where I was from, I knew how to FEEL the thousands of miles beginning to grow inside my heart, because I began to feel lost in this definition known as "home."

Distanced.

Disconnected.

...But I was not assigned homework.

Because in fact, my homework became my life.

At home I gained these tiny bits of knowledge that I would hungrily grasp at, because these stories were the nourishment that would feed my soul.

Even though these stories of the Philippines were not filled with sugary sweet gumdrops of this fairytale land that I had once concocted as a young girl, they were instead filled with the same salty tears that had been shed when my mother lovingly handed me to her sister years ago in hopes that I would never taste the same pain and hunger that had left her starving for something more.

My mother made a grave mistake, sending me across the globe to this place that had only taught me how to point back at where I came from.

I have become a healer.

Repairing

The distance.

The connections.

Reframing the way that I define home.

Home may very well be where the heart is and it doesn't have to be one fairy tale compared to the other, because my home, my heart, is made up of the salty tears, the sugary sweet gum drops and everything in between that has formed the dots that hash out every mile that connects me to where I'm from, where I am now, and where I am going.

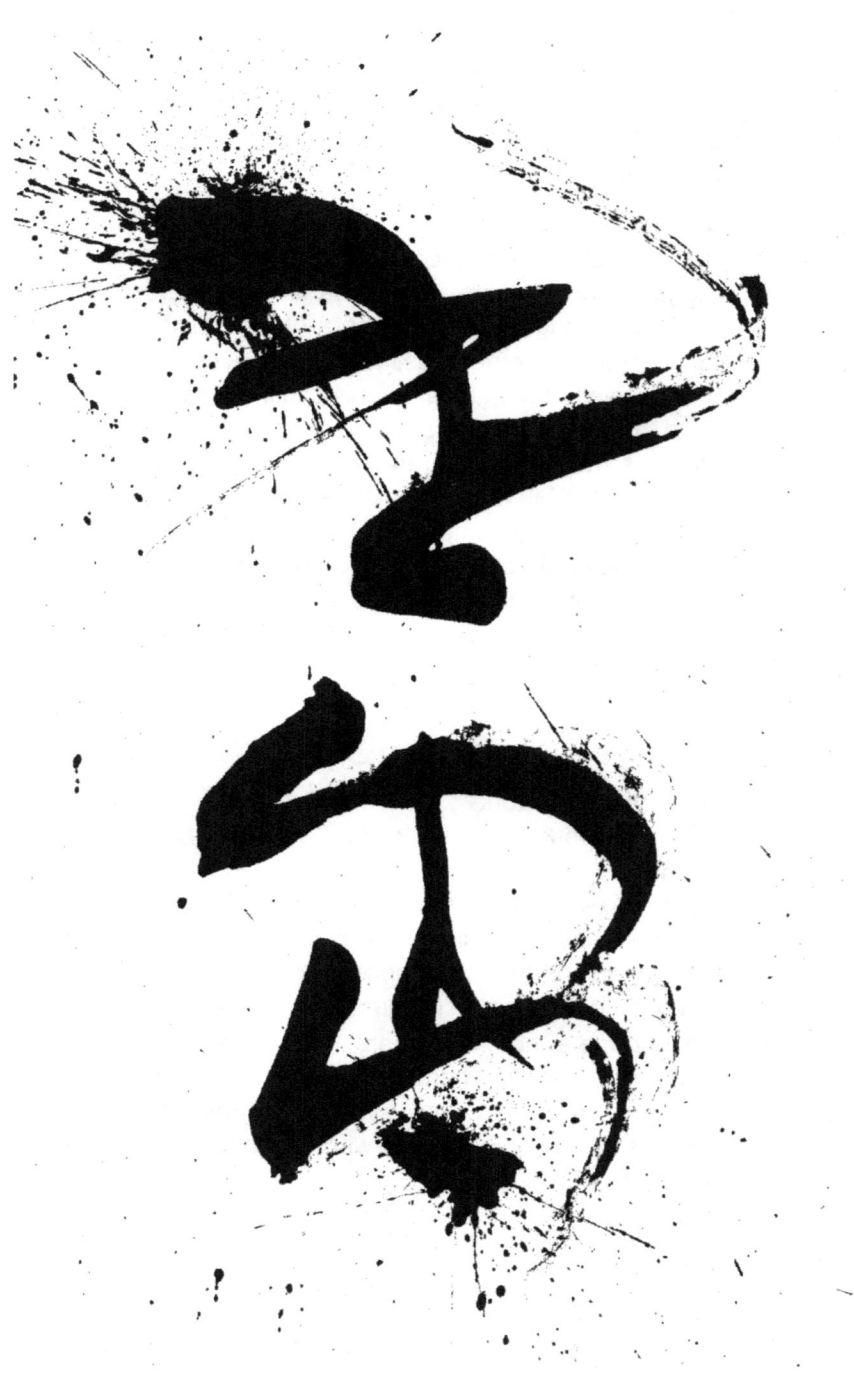

Ako - Me

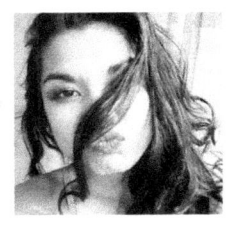

Lara
Calgary, Canada

My name is Lara, and I come with quite a mixed background. My mother is Filipina and my father is South Indian, my own hometown being in Abu Dhabi, UAE. All my life I've had a hard time identifying or labeling what I am, or where I'm from. Being mixed, I've always felt like I'm everything and nothing at the same time. For some reason people always feel the need to tell me who I am - either I wasn't Pinay enough, Indian enough, or I didn't have a legal right to call myself "from" the UAE. I've always found it frustrating, having some sort of identity confusion as to who I am. Although many girls I know would love to be mixed blooded because it's the "in" thing or considered "exotic", I think there are many downsides to it that people don't realize. Take the language factor, for example. Mixed kids are often raised in a house that is a crossroad of cultures, the result being that they don't strongly grasp any one whole culture, nor do they don't end up learning the mother/father tongue. Although I know some words from each language, I don't fluently speak Tagalog, Hindi (or any other Filipino/Indian languages) nor do I speak any dialect of Arabic. A language is the gateway into a culture, and because I know none of my three languages, many people have considered me an outsider of those cultures. Not only that, but when people ask me "where I'm from" - it's almost as if they don't ask the right question. I'm aware that what they actually mean is "what's your ethnicity", but when someone asks me "where I'm from", I'm inclined to say where I'm born and raised - Abu Dhabi, UAE. I've always wished I could just give one straight answer like pure blooded people can, but in order to answer that question it feels like I'm telling a novel. Over the years I've gotten pretty used to quickly saying "I'm from UAE but I'm half Filipina half Indian", hoping to avoid any further curious questions but often enough I get the "So where are you really from? What side are you closest with? What languages do you speak?" or "So you're not really _____ (insert label here)" and sometimes even the odd "How did your parents meet, then?" To me, all of this is frustrating because I shouldn't feel the need to justify myself or my culture to anyone, and yet I have to regularly.

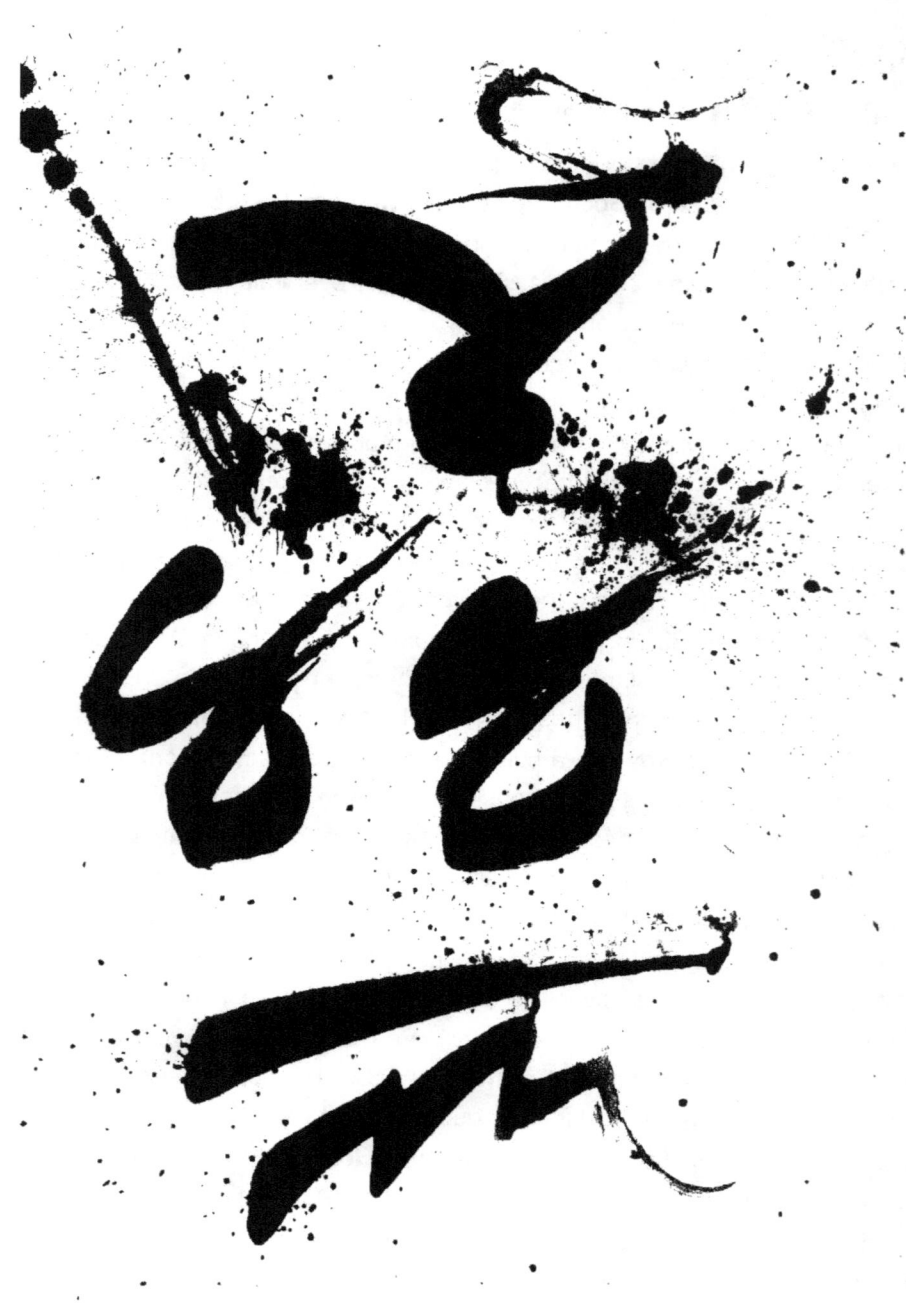

Pagtitiis - Patience

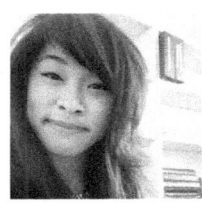

Jessica
Daly City, California, USA

My first long term relationship was physically and mentally abusive, leaving me to feel very alone and insecure. These thoughts consumed me, leading me to abuse my body and commit a failed suicide attempt. I felt that God had granted me a second chance of life and that I was meant to live for a bigger purpose, so seized the opportunity to end my relationship while long distance. As I struggled through a deep depression and episodes of panic attacks after the break up, I committed myself to social justice and found my own ways to heal through community work, activism, and empowering individuals through a Pinayist pedagogy. Years later, I discovered that my ex boyfriend shot his girlfriend and himself. I felt numb upon hearing the news and thought, "that could've been me." But if I had not gathered the strength to pull myself out of my lowest low, I would've never found the community that has inspired my work and the group of people who I call family. Kung walang tiyaga, walang nilaga.

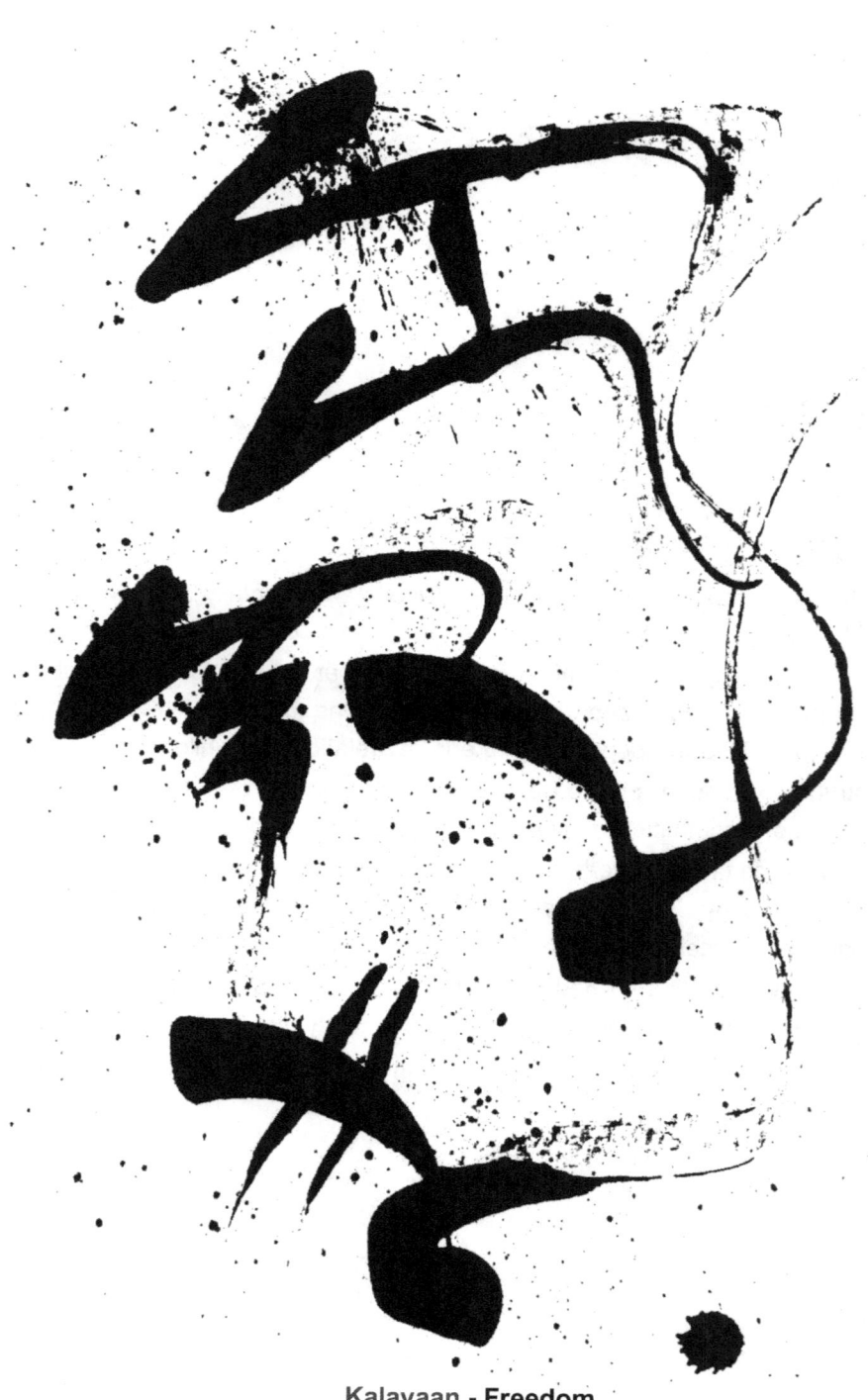

Kalayaan - Freedom

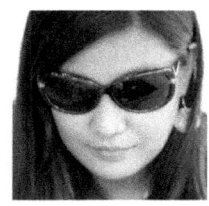

Red Lady
Pismo Beach, California, USA

I say Ka-La-Ya-A. Freedom if I may, following the baybayin characters from ancients of ancients. The word that has been hard to utter for so many years growing up behind the bars of fear, guilt and shame. Accustomed with the system of organized groups, religions and factions, it has definitely been difficult for me to even look at myself in the mirror and tell myself—I am free.

A follower of the elder, I have grown being too scared of what other people might think about every minute detail there is in my everyday routine. I've gone crazy from the point of whether I was getting good grades at school, down to whether I was brushing my teeth in the right direction. Yes, definitely crazy. It was once misconstrued as obsessive compulsive. Oh well, the interpretations vary from one's perspective to another, I guess. My world was home, school and church. They say go to church or go to jail? That was me going to church right there. Pretty interesting life, isn't it?

Years have gone by until I have voluntarily rebelled against the subtle exploitations of the jungle where I once belonged. My immediate forebears have considered it too radical, too left. Others would consider it progressive, extreme and out of control. Well, I consider it FREEDOM.

At a time when I have actually realized liberty, it was indeed extreme, but it was the "perfect freedom" that I've always wanted. My preferences have changed to the point where I barely turn on the television and have gotten into some serious reading about your non-mainstream brain food that you would never ever find in your typical bookstore. The visibility of my old fashioned side is still there, but I guess I am free to do that too.

Apart from carrying the smiling effect of a woman who appreciates a simple sunset or the start at night, I'm still in search of depth. I like deep conversations that help me learn. I love to learn and I am glad I am finally free to learn and not held up by the resources that were just force fed on me.

The lack of freedom and the realization of freedom definitely opened avenues for awareness, passion and deep happiness.

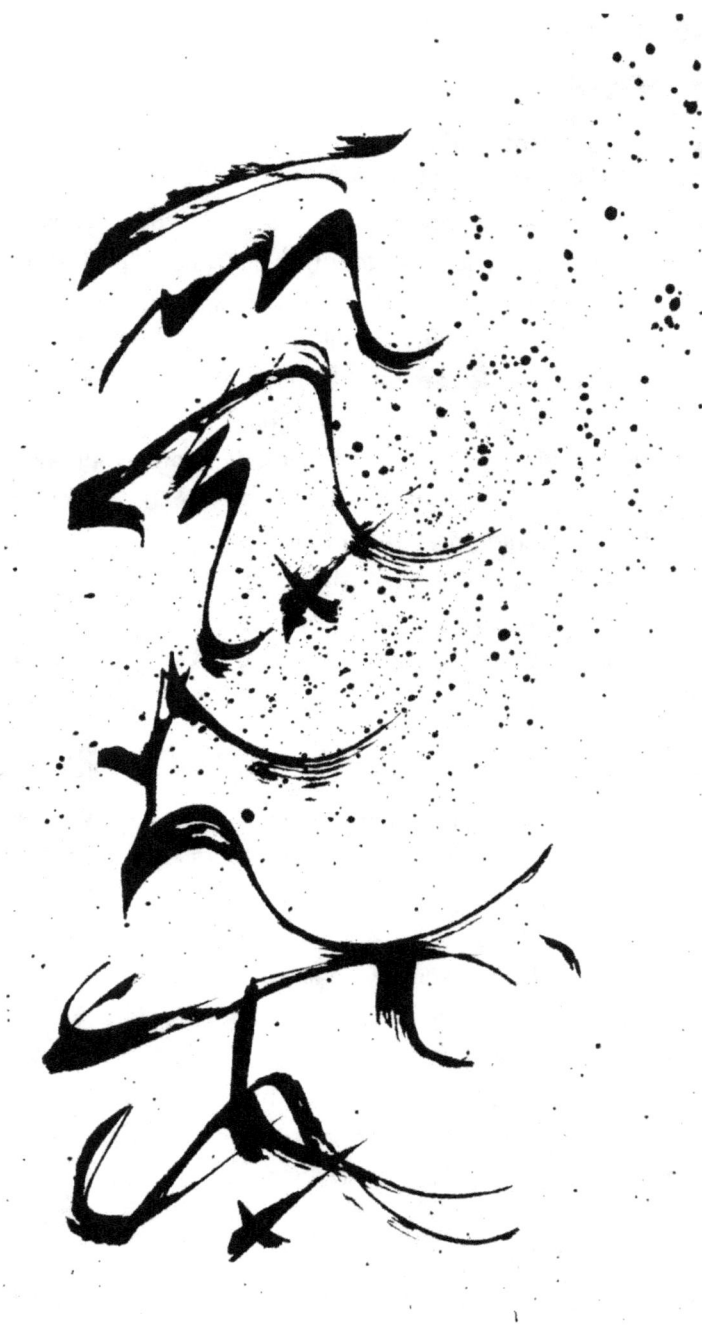

Indak - Dance

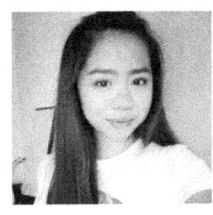

Ria
Perth, Australia

Indak is a Tagalog word for dance. Life is a dance, and so is love. Our body and soul need to be connected for the dance to be beautiful; there needs to be an invisible bond that connects everything together. Just like in life, we need to connect to everything around us. Just like in love, we need to connect to the person we're in love with.

We are fragile at some point or another, and that just explains how sometimes we are afraid to dance with someone; afraid that they may step on our feet or we might step on theirs. We're afraid to get hurt. But sometimes, we just can't resist the beat of the music, the beat of the heart.

And so, everyday we practice and practice to perfect that dance of life, that dance of love.

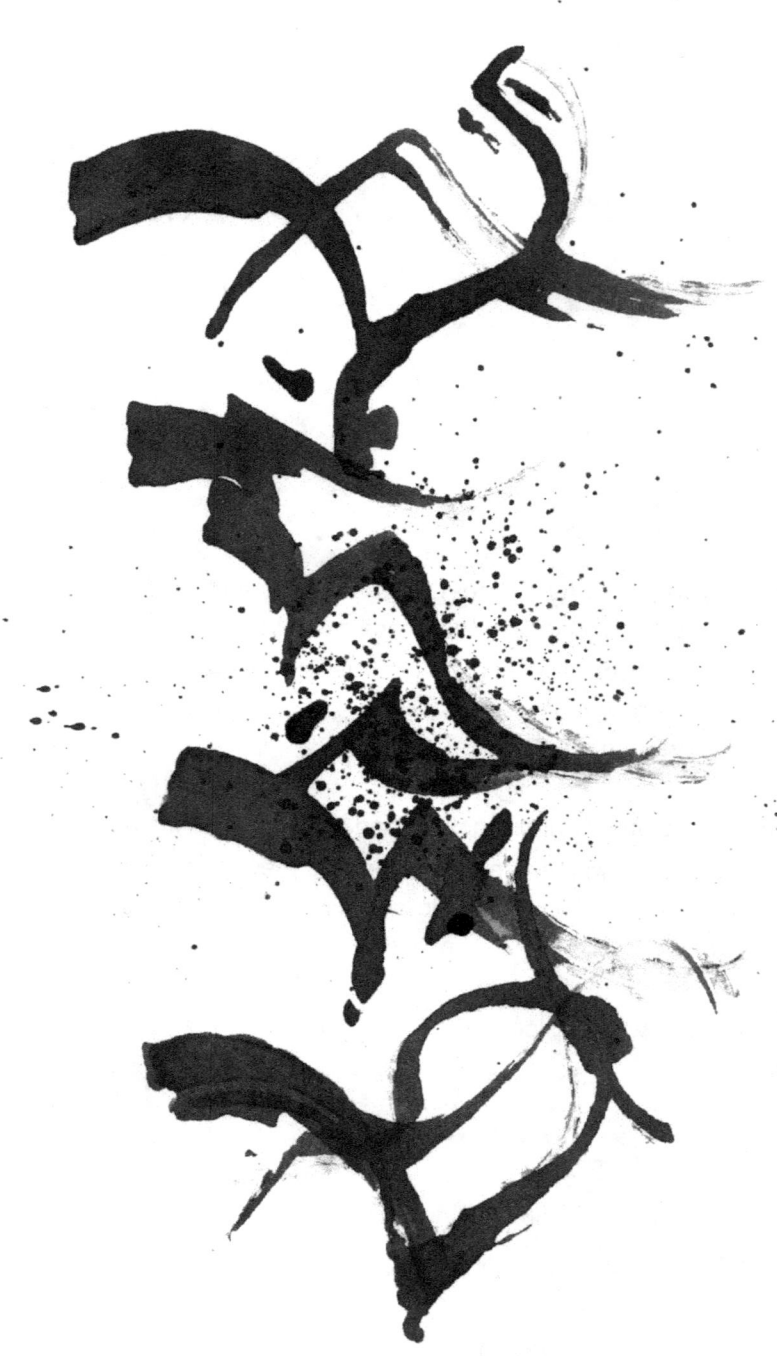

Mandirigma - Warrior

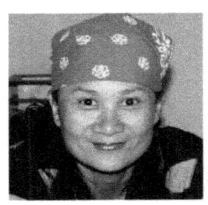

Charina
Palo Alto, California, USA

I was born and raised in the Philippines. I was raped twice. I self-destructed with drugs and alcohol. This past June 10, 2013, I've been sober, off drugs and alcohol for 13 years. My sister died last September 1, 2011 and I did not drink or use over that. A warrior is someone who has defied the insanity and pain in in this so-called LIFE. I am a survivor, no matter what. I am proud to say, I live life to the fullest with the help of my AA, Friends and My Amazing Family, who love me unconditionally. I heal others through my Perseverance. ROAR!!!!!!!!!

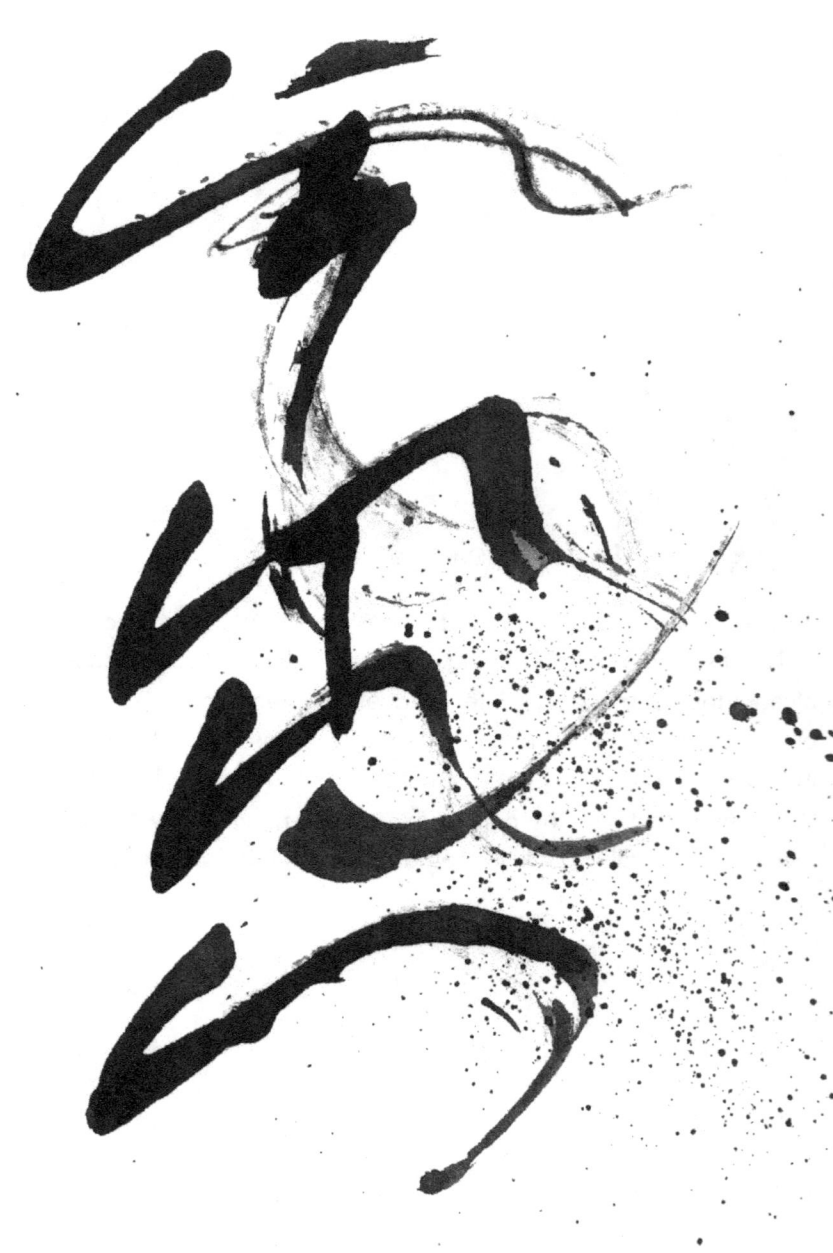

Likha - Create

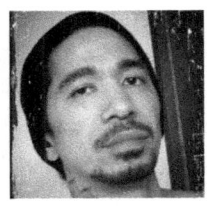

Don "Catfish"
American Canyon, California, USA
Instagram: catfish30

I chose this word because it has always been my life endeavor since I was a young boy in the Philippines. I never had a father to give me toys or who can afford to buy one. I never look at it as a sad phase in my life but as a spark! My Lolo was the one who sparked my mind by giving me a recycled brown pan de sal paper, saying, "if you can't have something then create something." From then on, I create something from whatever I have, or recreate it to make something better. Imagination played a big part in it also. My vision of how or what I created strengthens my resilience to head forward in what I do. As time passes through, I never looked at failures or mistakes; to me they are guides to make things better for tomorrow. Success to me is the ability to create and recreate.

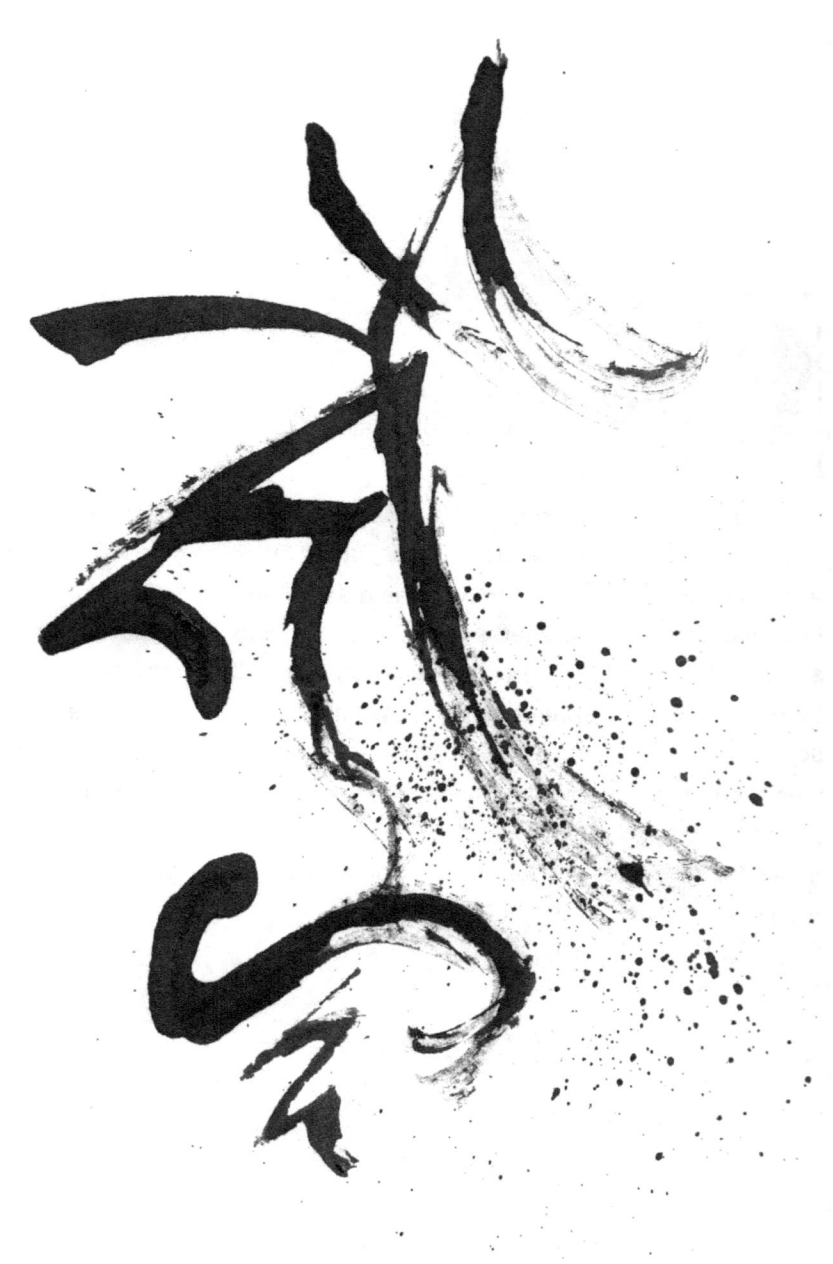

Panahon - Season

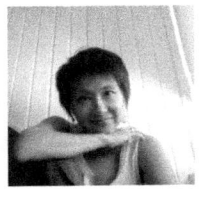

Claire
Singapore
Twitter: cam_writes

Where I grew up, there are four seasons. Then at 14 I began a life of moving from country to country. Much as I dream of the alternative - staying in one place my whole life - it isn't long before I imagine living somewhere else, for a season or more. The fragments that make up my moveable life are seasons, most of which last for years. The beauty of this thinking is that spring, summer, fall, and winter run on a loop, repeating with a comforting degree of predictability. Whether it's a return to places I've lived, or I've landed somewhere entirely unknown, the familiar finds me and I find where the new has overlapped. I've grown too, of course. But the sameness comes back, so I am home wherever I am.

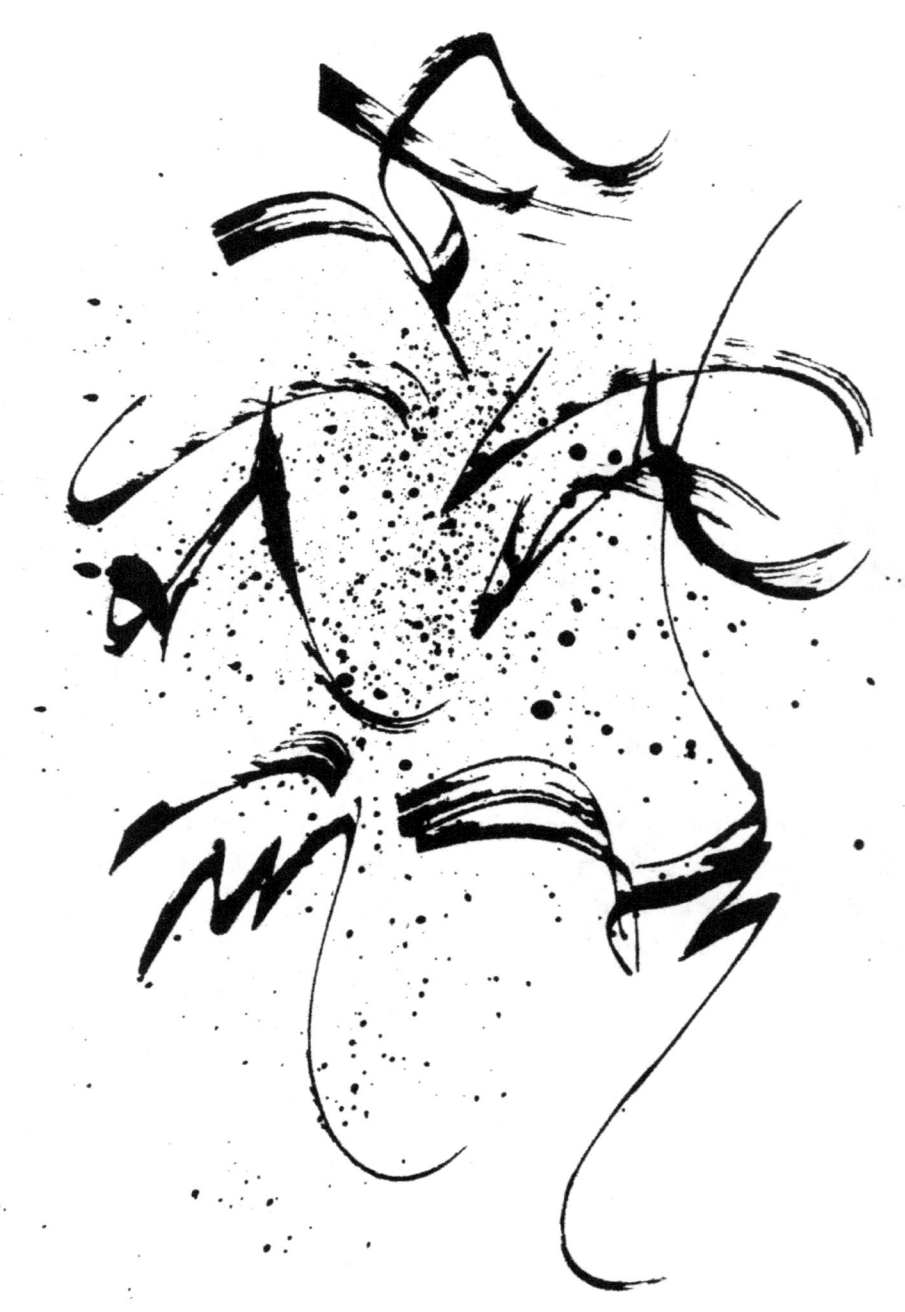

Pagkakaisa - Unity

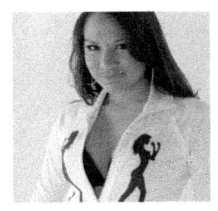

Tamara "Miss Rara"
Stockton, California, USA
missrara.com

On September 26th, 2009, typhoon Ondoy, one of the most destructive typhoons in Philippine history, hit the Philippines. It left 710 fatalities with starving families displaced from their home. Working in the Mixed Martial Arts industry, with experience in event planning, I knew I could make a difference. More importantly, I knew that WE as a Filipino community could make a difference. I went to The Underground, an MMA forum, and made a thread titled "What can we do to help?" From then on ideas started rolling in and big names in the MMA and Filipino community started to come on board like Brandon Vera, Mark Munoz, Shane Del Rosario, Romy Adanza, Arianny Celeste, TapouT, Fight Chix, Legends MMA Training Center, Fil-Am Arts, Kababayan LA, Little Manila Foundation, etc. Next thing you know, Their Fight Is Our Fight (TFIOF) was created, an event with demonstrations, seminars, and autograph signings to help raise money for the typhoon victims in the Philippines. Their Fight Is Our Fight made history with its first Filipino-American MMA event on October 26th, 2009 - Filipino American history month. We raised over $3,000 for the Philippine Red Cross that day. And it could not have happened without our compadres amongst our Filipino MMA community. That's why I chose the word "Pagkakaisa"; we are one in alliance and unity, just as our *manong*s and *manang*s taught us.

Their Fight Is Our Fight made history with its first Filipino-American MMA event on October 26th, 2009 - Filipino American history month. We raised over $3,000 for the Philippine Red Cross that day. And it could not have happened without our compadres amongst our Filipino MMA community. That's why I chose the word "Pagkakaisa", we are one in alliance and unity, just as our manongs and manangs taught us.

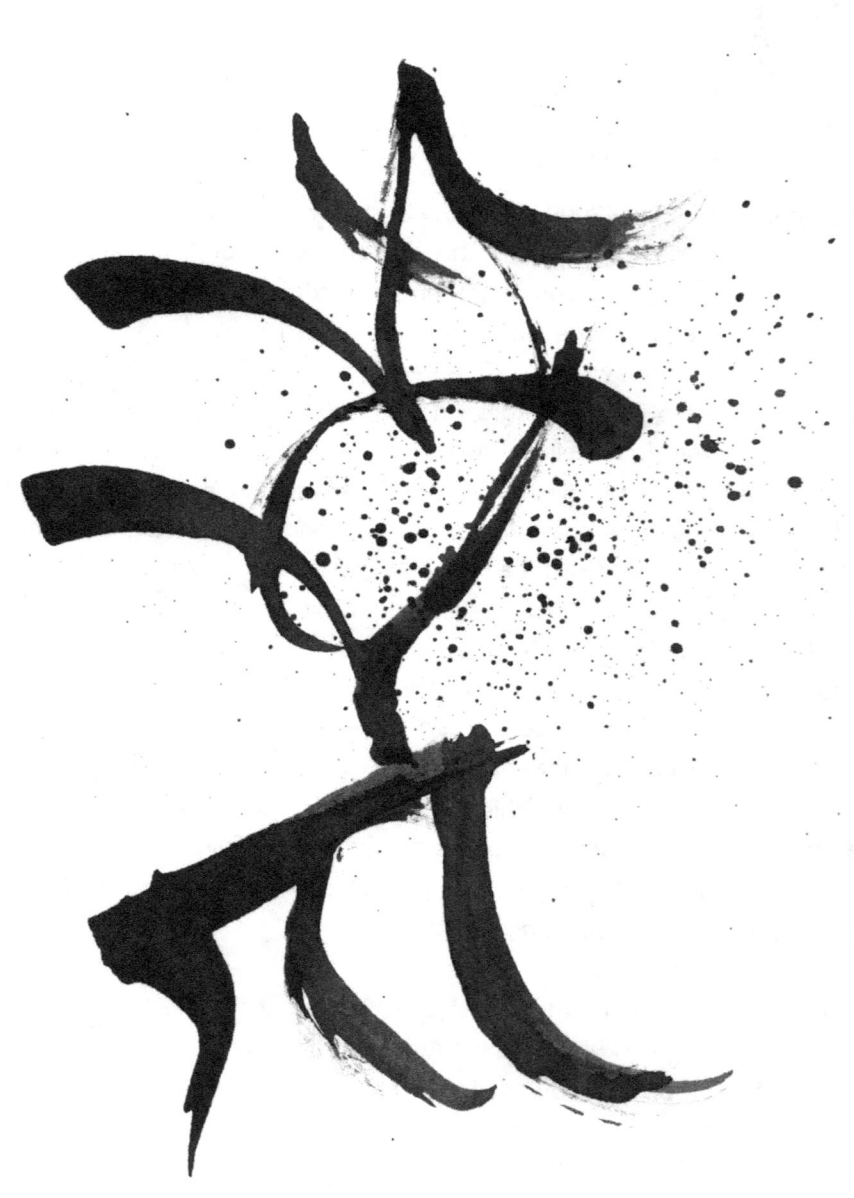

Pamana - Heritage

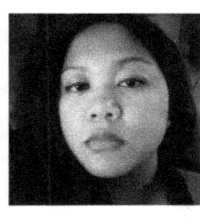

Bernadette
San Francisco, California, USA
Instagram: fatlaces

Born to fight to belong in America as a Filipina, learned to protect my family and honor my heritage. Heart. Mind. Spirit.

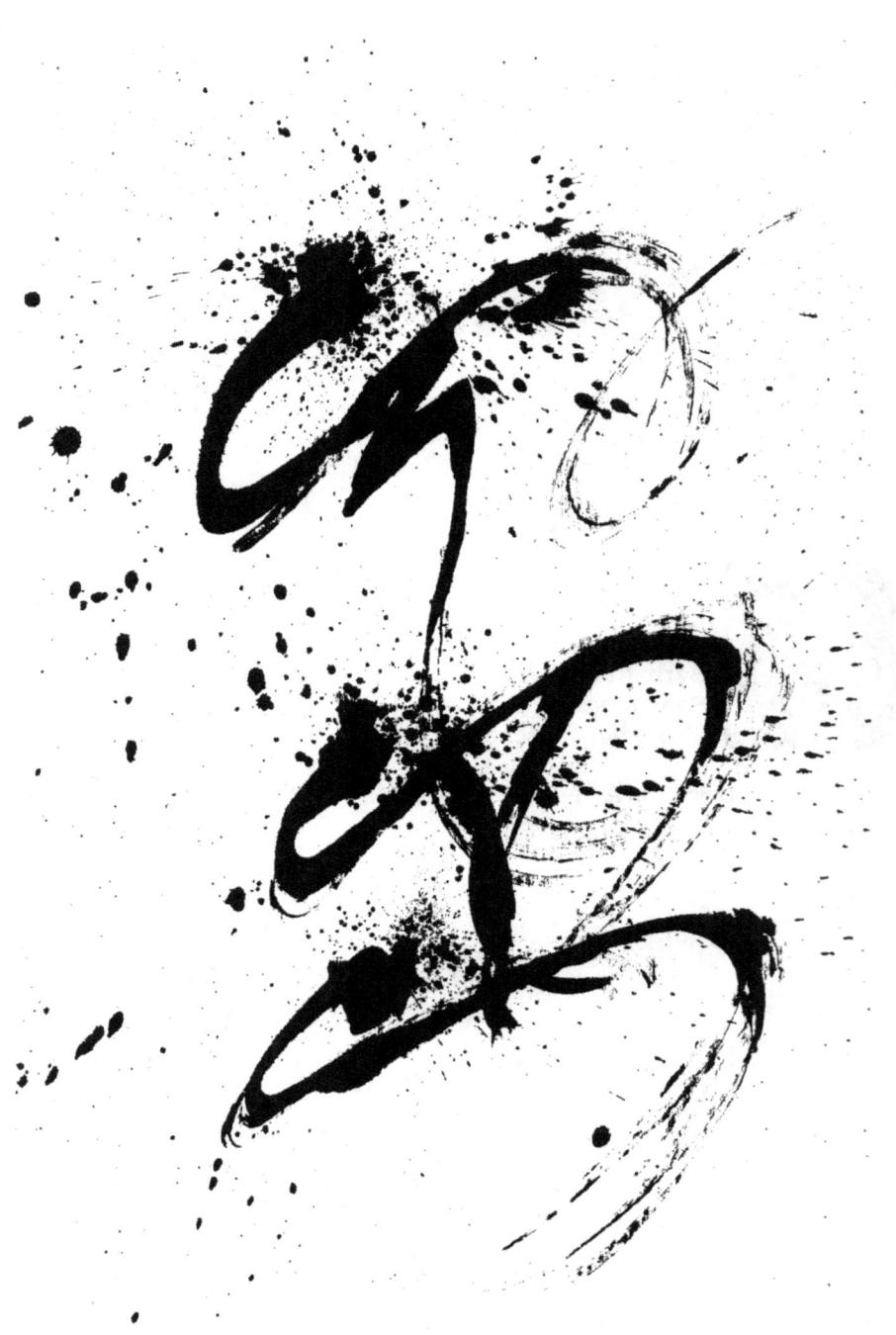

Lakas - Strength

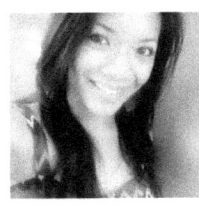

April
Waipahu, Hawaii, USA

When I was a young girl I was sexually assaulted by someone who I trusted. After that, I was scarred. I became angry and numb. I changed. I realized that I didn't want to stay angry. I told myself that things will get better. I had told myself to stay strong. It took me several years to gain confidence and to trust others. There's been several other experiences where I had the choice to stay strong or to give up. I chose to stay strong. Physical strength is good. However, being strong mentally and emotionally is what keeps us sane. This word is a reminder to myself to always stay strong no matter what.

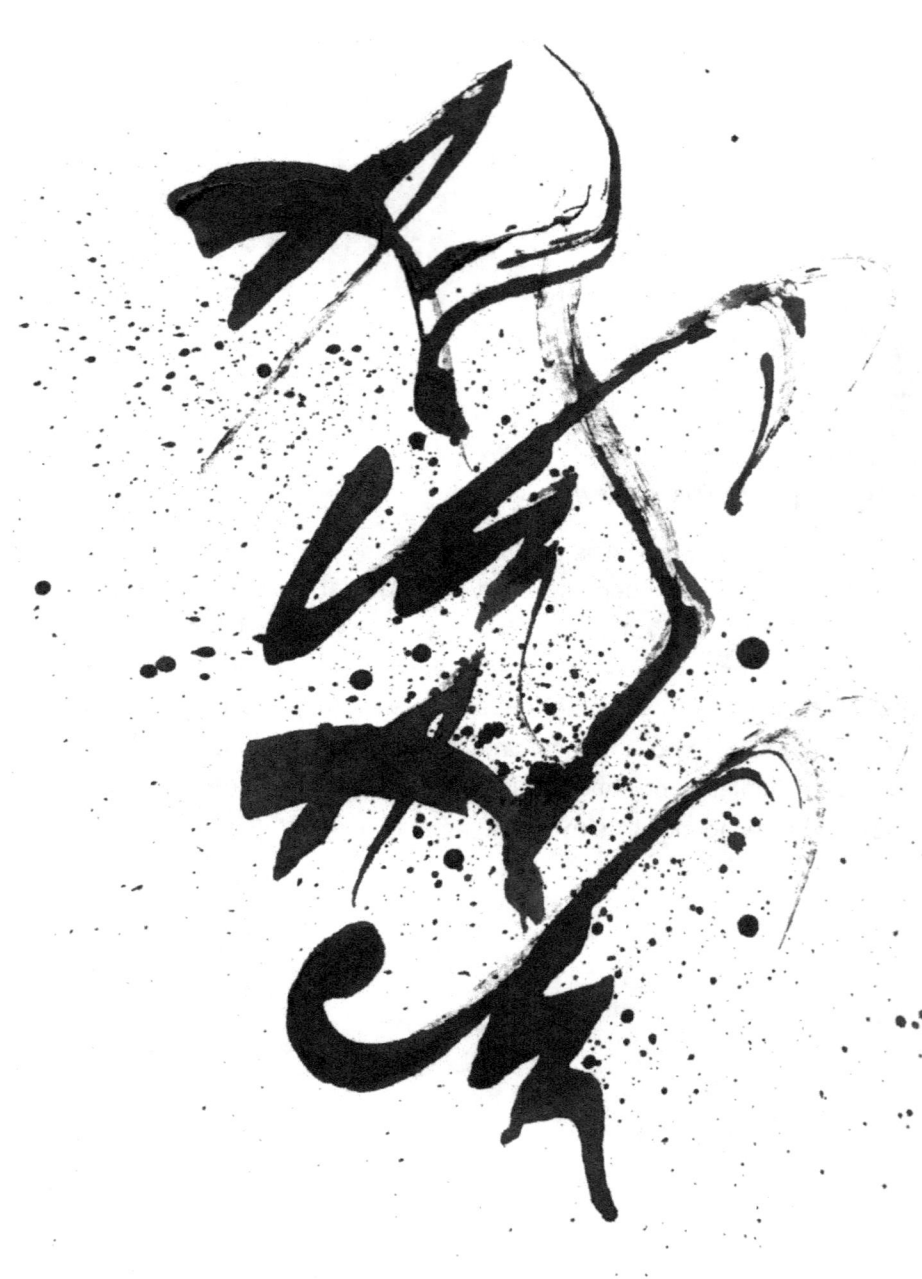

Ala'ala - Memory

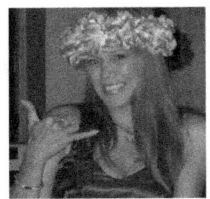

Jacquiline
Huntsville, Alabama, USA

I chose this word because I am a Filipina, born and raised in various cities of the Philippines. I was raised there till I was 15, in my 3rd year of high school (Saint Joseph Catholic School in Olongapo City). Then went to the U.S to live the remainder of my life to this day. I love my country, I am supposed to love my people, but I can never forgive them for treating me like I did not belong (I am mestiza,half-white and half-Filipina, who speaks,reads and writes the language), so my skin was always lighter, my hair did not look like a what Filipina should have. I was always rejected in groups or cliques when I was younger, and often went off playing on my own, thinking to myself, WHY? "I eat like them, I act like them, I speak like them. Why don't they play with me? And for some reason, I found ways to earn friendship, not through kindness but through money and material things, which got to me more and more. It sickens me each day growing up that I found it so hard to find a friend who was with me for ME. To this day I found ,even here in United States, the mentality of the ones I truly care about who are Filipino still act like that towards me at this day and age. There were false hopes in my head growing up, that... it was only happening because of those kids, or people in that specific place, that I will face another journey when I got to America - That I would fit in here, for I am light-skinned with   light brown hair, light brown eyes. BOY WAS I WRONG. Here in the U.S. I am not light enough, my hair not light enough, and so on and so forth. It took a long time for me to learn to stop buying friends and to accept people for who they are and move on. I have a lot of associates but never found that "one true friend". I guess I will always be a misfit, no matter where I go. But that's okay, because I realized something about myself: that I am UNIQUELY ONE-OF-A-KIND ~ coming from a beautiful place with countless islands and thousands of people who look the same? I am one-in-a-million, a diamond in the rut, and GOD LOVES ME LIKE THAT!

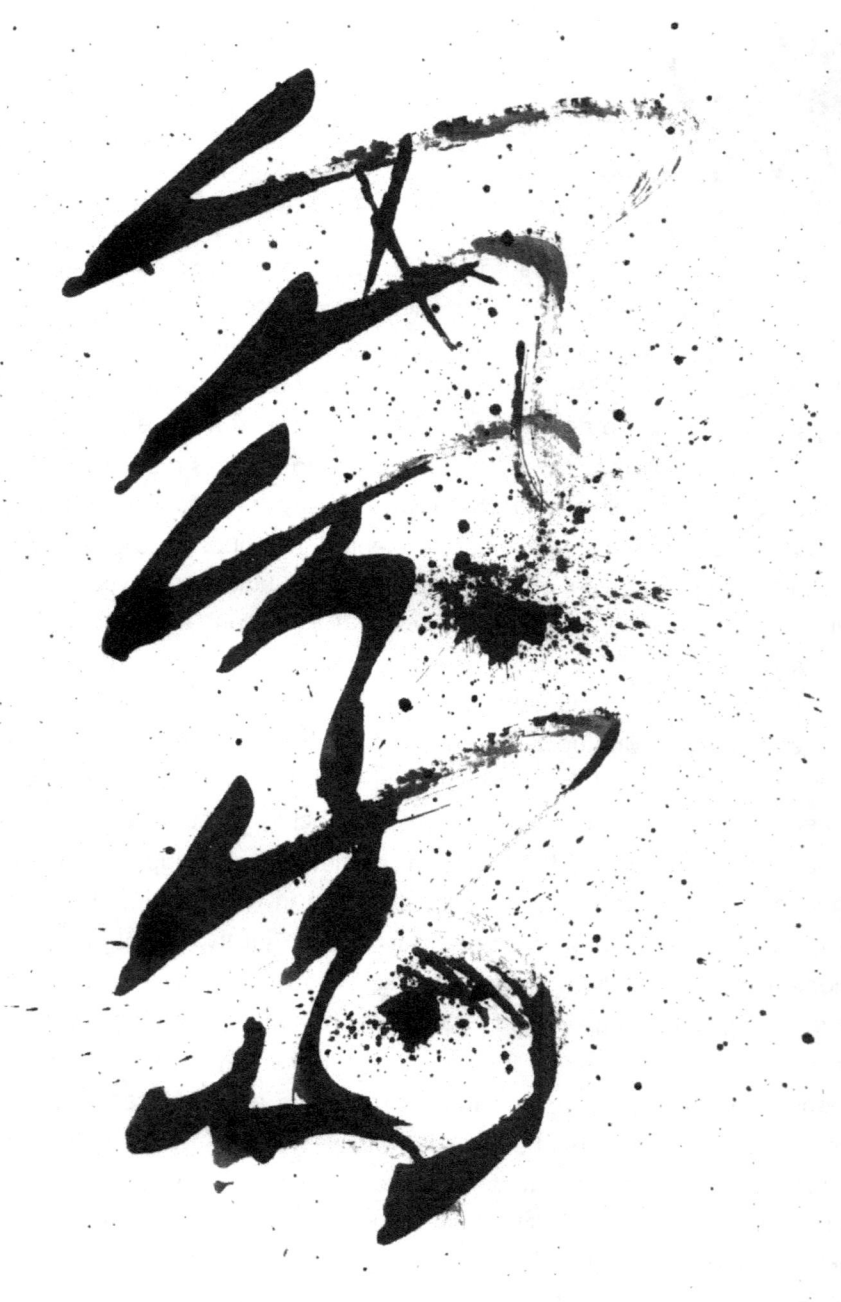

Kaluluwa - Soul

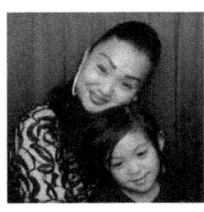

Rae
Los Angeles, California, USA

I grew up as a first generation Fil-Am and I have always had my family growing up. Although we have always been together, and of course we have similarities, I always had a lot of conflict between what I felt was being true to myself, and what my family wanted. I was always seen as the outspoken and rebellious one in the family and ended up marrying outside of our culture. My family told me they liked my husband but their actions said otherwise. My husband is not Filipino and grew up totally different. He had no family and had a very rough childhood. Because of this, he was very independent-minded. He encouraged me to think outside the box and follow what I had been fighting inside for so long. Although my husband is not my blood family, he is the one who helped me be true to myself. My husband and four children are my everything. They are part of my soul and I wouldn't change a thing!

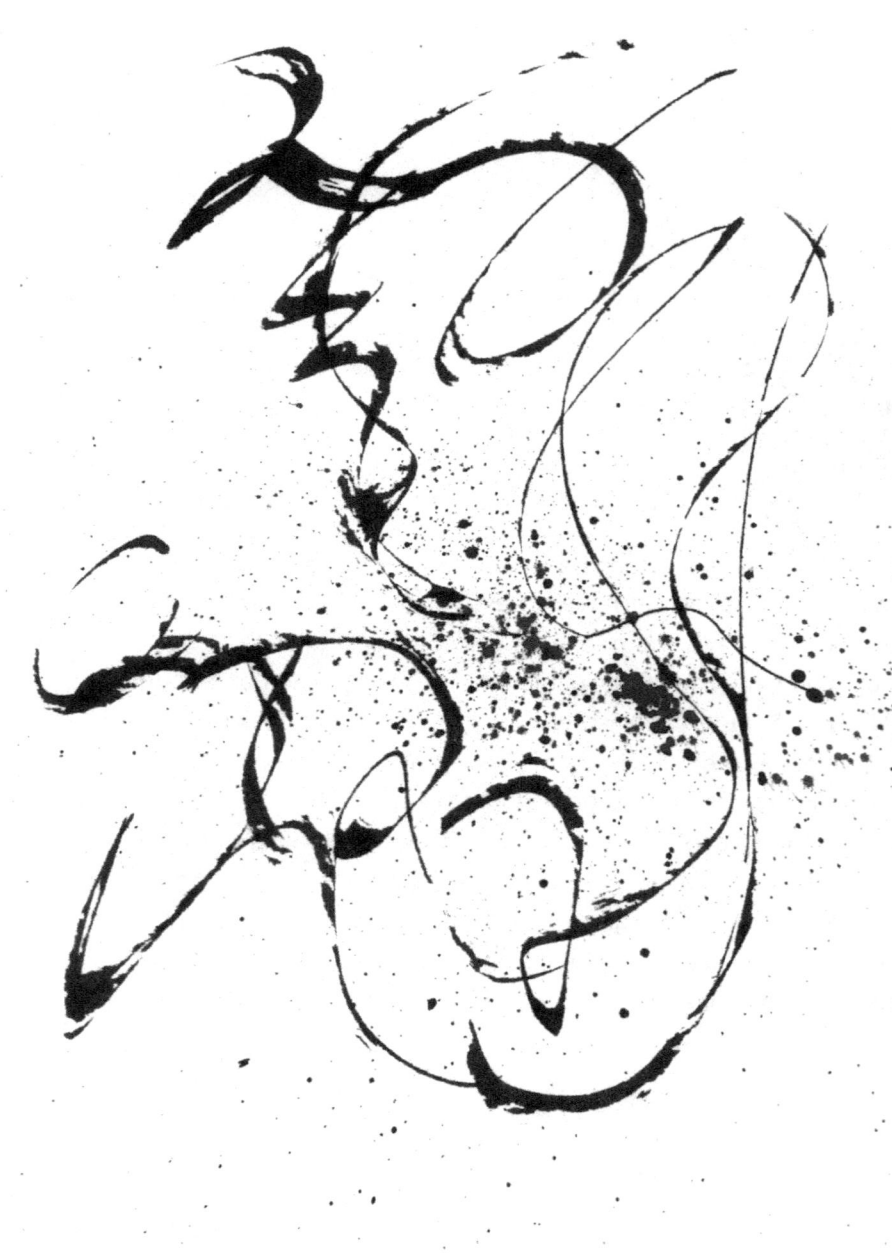

Lakay - Old man

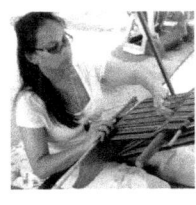

Holly
San Francisco, California, USA
Kalingafornia-laga.com

In 2008, while traveling in the Cordilleras, I heard, "when is the baket (old woman) leaving?" ~ we all laughed, but my shortened breath while hiking made it impossible for me to visit Whang Od, the 92-year-old traditional Kalinga tattoo artist ~ my grandmother Mary Caluza Calica, called her dark, humble, quiet and considerate husband, Blas Cacdac Calica, "lakay" (old man). ~ he never called her baket, it wasn't in his character ~ so funny this word stands out so much for me ~ it's truly napintas (beautiful) as it replays those beautiful memories of my grandparents who lived in the Fillmore before eminent domain, the Haight Ashbury before gentrification permanently changed each neighborhood, and the Richmond districts of San Francisco bringing diversity as they snuck onto tennis courts before sunrise to rally with each other ~ her wit and domineering leadership and his humble strength and kindness for our family stamped into my consciousness through eternity ~

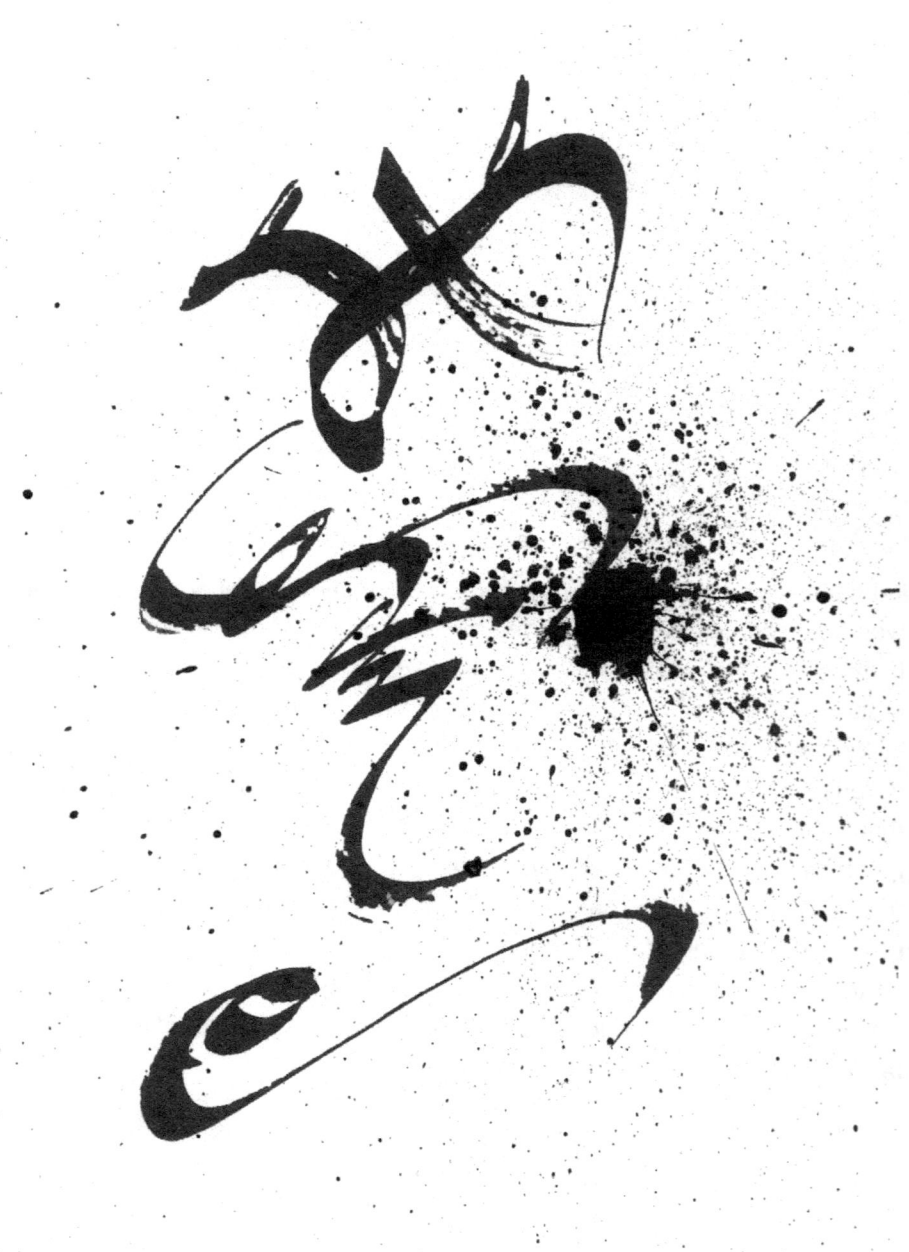

Paglanghap - Inspiration

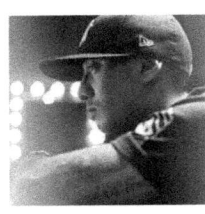

Joel
Manila, Philippines
Pandptattoo.com

Before starting P&P tattoo I did a lot of research on different tattoo shops in the US. The one I loved the most was the ever-famous LA INK or HIGH VOLTAGE TATTOO, which was made famous by Kat Von D. I was so amazed with the shop. I decided to get the word "inspiration" tattooed on me, as I was so inspired by their place and hoped that when I build my tattoo business in the Philippines it would one day just like that shop I went to in LA. That was 2008 and now its 2013 and I recently opened my 4th branch of P&P tattoo here in the Philippines. A lot of people say that we are the #1 tattoo shop in the Philippines, but all I know is that I always kept myself inspired and motivated to reach my goals.

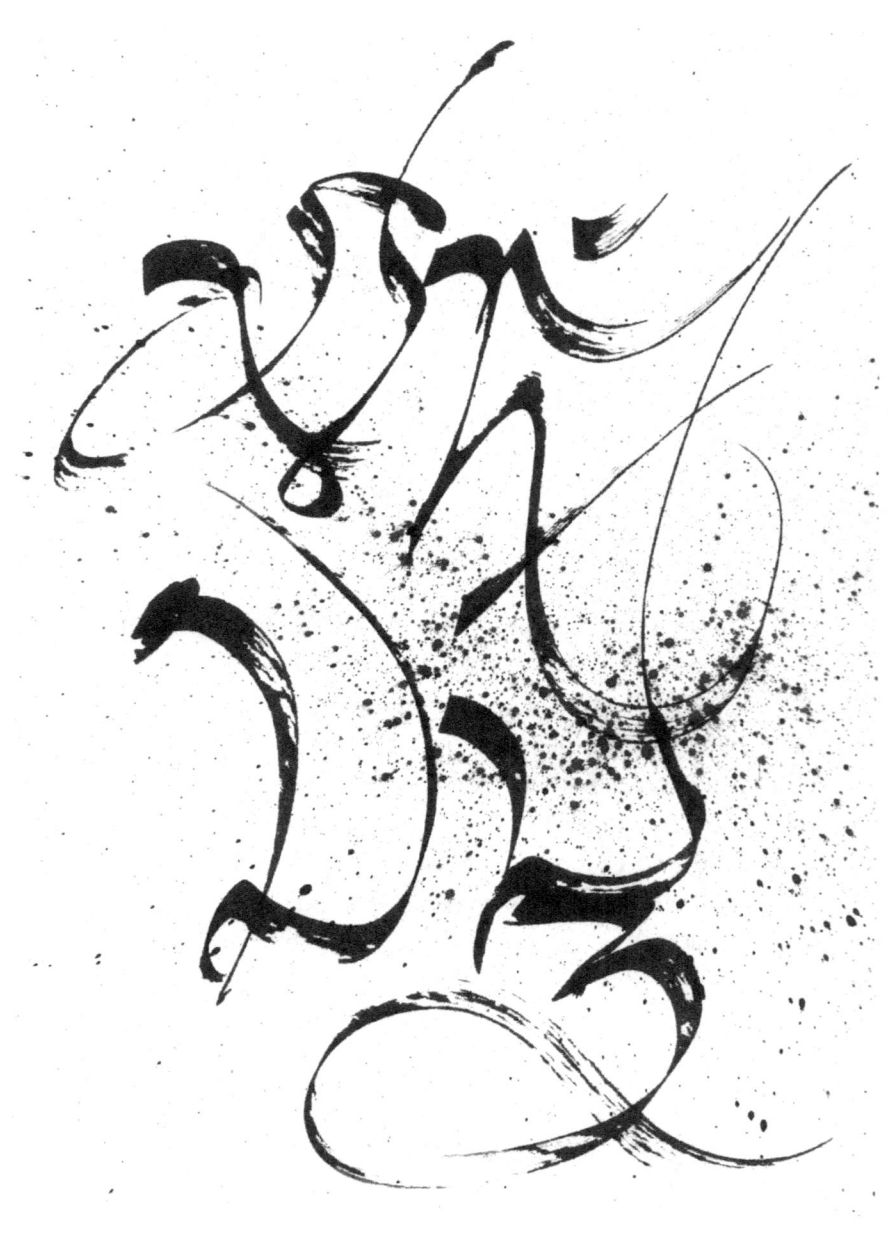

Mariwasa - Rich

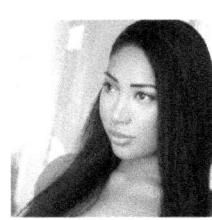

Ayvee Rose
Los Angeles, California, USA
Ayvee.me

Kumusta kumusta kumusta ingat ka lagi /kumusta kumusta ingat po
Kumusta kumusta kumusta ingat ka lagi /kumusta kumusta ingat po
Philippines 150 degrees/ I'm underneath the palm trees /eating mangosteen
Jump up in the jeepney /got some people to see/ wishing I be ice cold freezing AC
One cousin I know got a whole room full of it/ just cut the button on and the air box blowing it I'm bout to get my nails did at pinkie rice girl's crib/ manicure pedicure sick french tips Tonight everybody coming by for videoki/ in the front yard on an old school TV

The sun go down low the breeze start blowing/ here in DDS city Kumusta kumusta kumusta ingat ka lagi /kumusta kumusta ingat po Kumusta kumusta kumusta ingat ka lagi /kumusta kumusta ingat po I'm gonna be Air Con Rich/ I'm gonna be Air Con Rich

I'm gonna be Air Con Rich/ I'm gonna be Air Con Rich
I'm gonna be Air Con Rich/ I'm gonna be Air Con Rich
I'm gonna be Air Con Rich/ I'm gonna be
I be bumping all my songs on a micro ipod /lime with the apple sign fly little knock off
Got a calling card text to meet my girls at G mall / cheng cheng won 200 pesos from the game show Walking on the streets don't nobody bother me/ neighborhood watch be them OG vigilantes

If a boy get caught up in a market robbery/ mangosteen could smear the streets so awfully I'm running with the dragonfly chasing butterflies/ for a early morning sunrise ride on kuya's motorbike
Every morning when I rise it's like I'm marang high

I'm bout to put my people on we gonna be air con fly
Kumusta kumusta kumusta ingat ka lagi /kumusta kumusta ingat po Kumusta kumusta kumusta ingat ka lagi /kumusta kumusta ingat po I'm gonna be Air Con Rich/ I'm gonna be Air Con Rich
We gonna be Air Con Rich/ Rich Rich Rich Rich Rich
Air Con Rich/ I'm gonna be Air Con Rich
I'm gonna be Air Con Rich/ I'm gonna be Air Con Rich

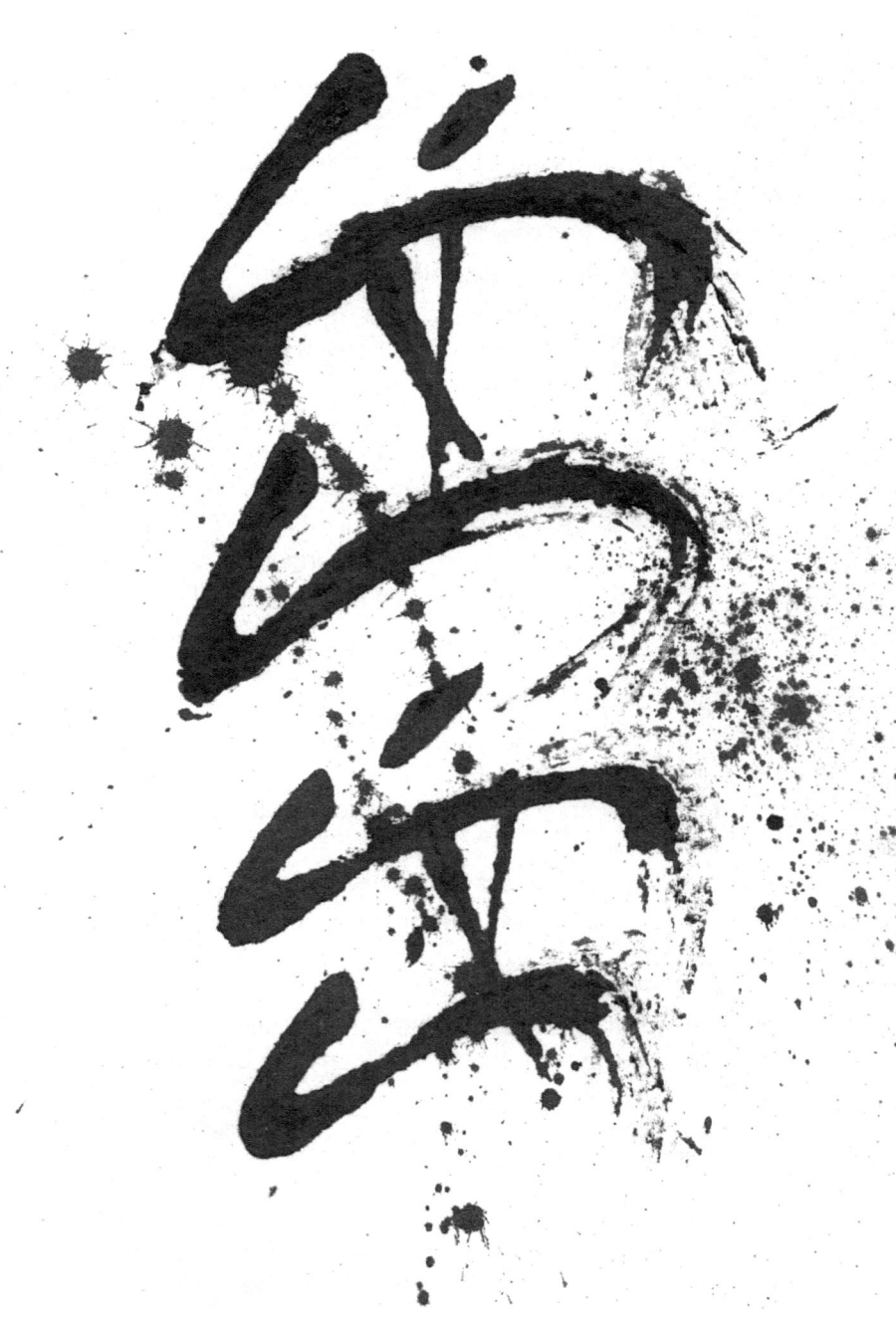

Kiki - Vagina

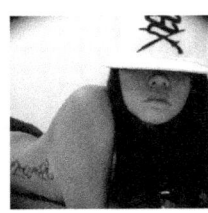

Tiffany
San Francisco, California, USA

Named of course by my mother, Kiki for me definitely has a persona of her own. I wouldn't go as far to say that she has matured but most definitely has evolved over time. One of my favorite moments that I like to share about her was Kiki's first encounter with identity theft. I was about seven years old and knew the one and only Kiki in the world was my very little miss "down there". Then the day came, I was at my auntie's house - my white auntie's house - and she started calling to my stepfather: "Kiki ... Kiki!!!" Immediately, I turned to my mother and said "Mom, Kiki? Kiki is...," where my mother, straight-faced Pinay said, "yes." In which I tried to clarify, "but auntie is calling dad Kiki!?!?" And again my mother, straight-faced Pinay, says "I know," and with my persistent self I ask, "Whyyyy is she calling him that???" As a true Pinay mother she doesn't alleviate my confusion and, probably laughing to herself, she responds again, straight-faced Pinay, "I don't know!" I was so dumbfounded I didn't know if my auntie was trying to tease my stepfather or if she decided to name him Kiki because he really was a vagina?!!??

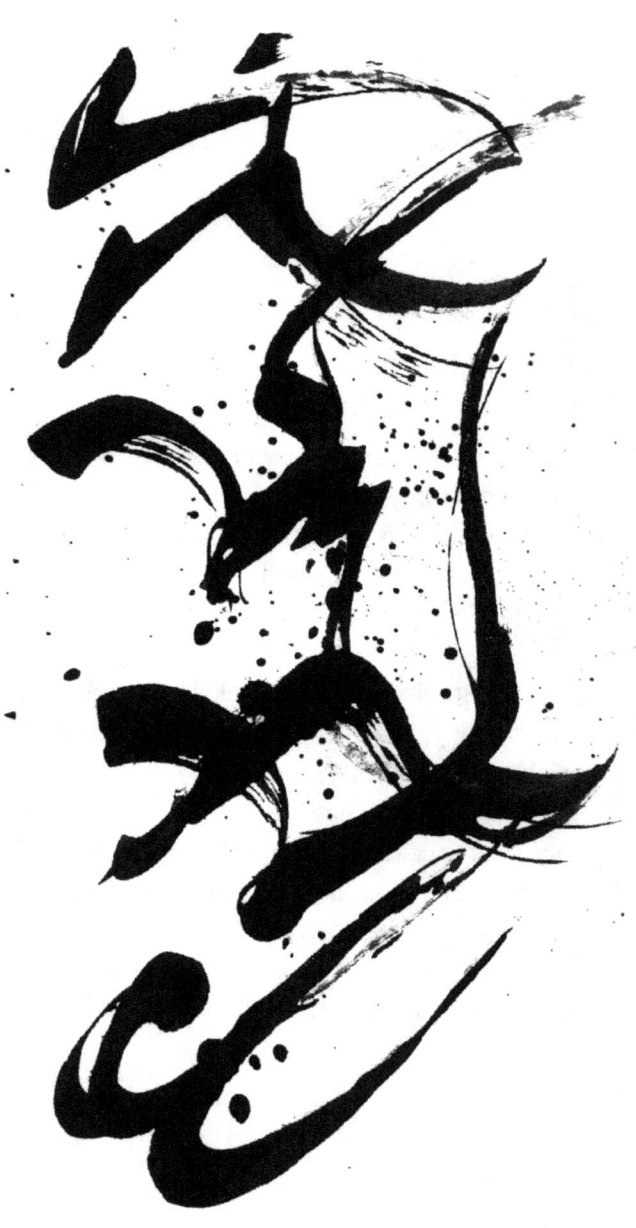

Kisapmata - Blink of an eye

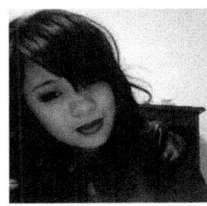

Aya
Las Vegas, Nevada, USA

Kisapmata. In the blink of an eye. People who know me can attest to this: I am a contemplative person. I think a lot, I over-think and over-analyze everything. I'm always in my head, constantly looking for answers to questions that don't deserve to be questions, seeking answers to my simple life's enigmas, searching for some form of order in my rhapsodic confusion of a mind. And inside this head there's a word that resonates confusion at all times, in varying hours of the day: Kisapmata.

In my twenty-three years of existence, I've learned this much: time doesn't wait for anyone, life is constantly changing, and that if you don't move fast enough, you get left behind. In this post-modern world we live in, getting left behind poses a lot of dilemma; and though life always brings with it a humongous load of obstacles we need to overcome, generally, I am one to be wary of them. One of my goals in life is this: to achieve the ever-elusive transcendence; that while I believe emotions are an essential part of living, they are something that needs to be overpowered in favor of more important things, like your goals and some life-changing decisions; that I stand by my belief that our senses and emotions limits our mind from experiencing real phenomena, thus making me want to learn how to transcend beyond what my eyes can see, what my ears can hear, what my nose can smell, what my tongue can taste, what my skin can feel, and what my hypothalamus is chronicling to my confused brain. And oh, how hard it is to achieve transcendence when everything around you seems to disappear in the blink of an eye. Kisapmata.

More than five years ago, I came to America, disheartened, but hopeful, and in search of a better future. Today, I am now a mother, and a patissier who's aspiring to change the world one dessert at a time. So much has happened to me in a span of five years. My whole world came crumbling down, and as my favorite author J.K. Rowling sums it up, "I was set free because my greatest fear have been realized, and I still had a daughter who I adore...and a big idea. And so rock bottom became a solid foundation on which I rebuilt my life." I could have succumbed to the darkness of what happened to me, and wallowed in woe, but I chose to be a bigger person and conquered my fears. And now, right at this moment, I could honestly say I haven't been this happy in my whole life. I have a loving daughter, a very supporting family, awesome friends, a job that I love, and I am on my way to the greatness I envisioned for myself. Life could be better, but I am happy, and that's all that matters, right? :)

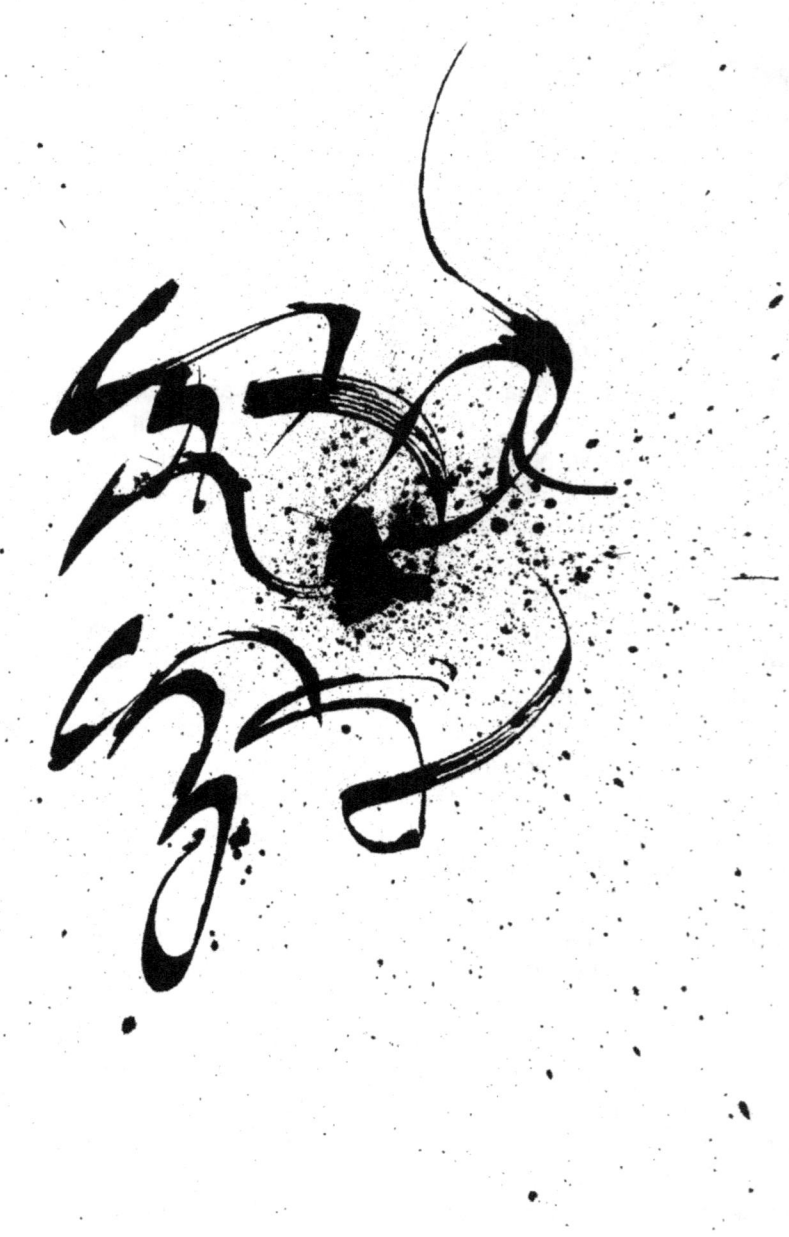

Kamalayan - Awareness

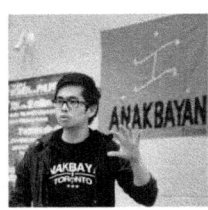

Ysh
Toronto, Ontario, Canada

Malay is the Tagalog word for awareness. If added with the "ka-" "-an" affixes, i.e. kamalayan, it does not only connote stream of consciousness. Kamalayan also means collective consciousness. One is described to be "may malay-tao" is he or she is awake.

It is in this awareness that I have inspiration to create art. My process is not to only express my cognitive state from which I recognize my existence as an individual. The constant challenge is how to act more deliberately through way of life, juxtaposing myself as an agent of change without drawing too much attention to my self— but to the knowledge that I am one in the collective. Being Filipino I recognize that "malay" also refers to the race under which I am classified. Yet I also act upon this knowledge by working with Anakbayan-Toronto, a comprehensive national democratic Filipino youth organization. We hold a series of activities called Kamalayan to uplift and inform young people of their crucial role in creating change.

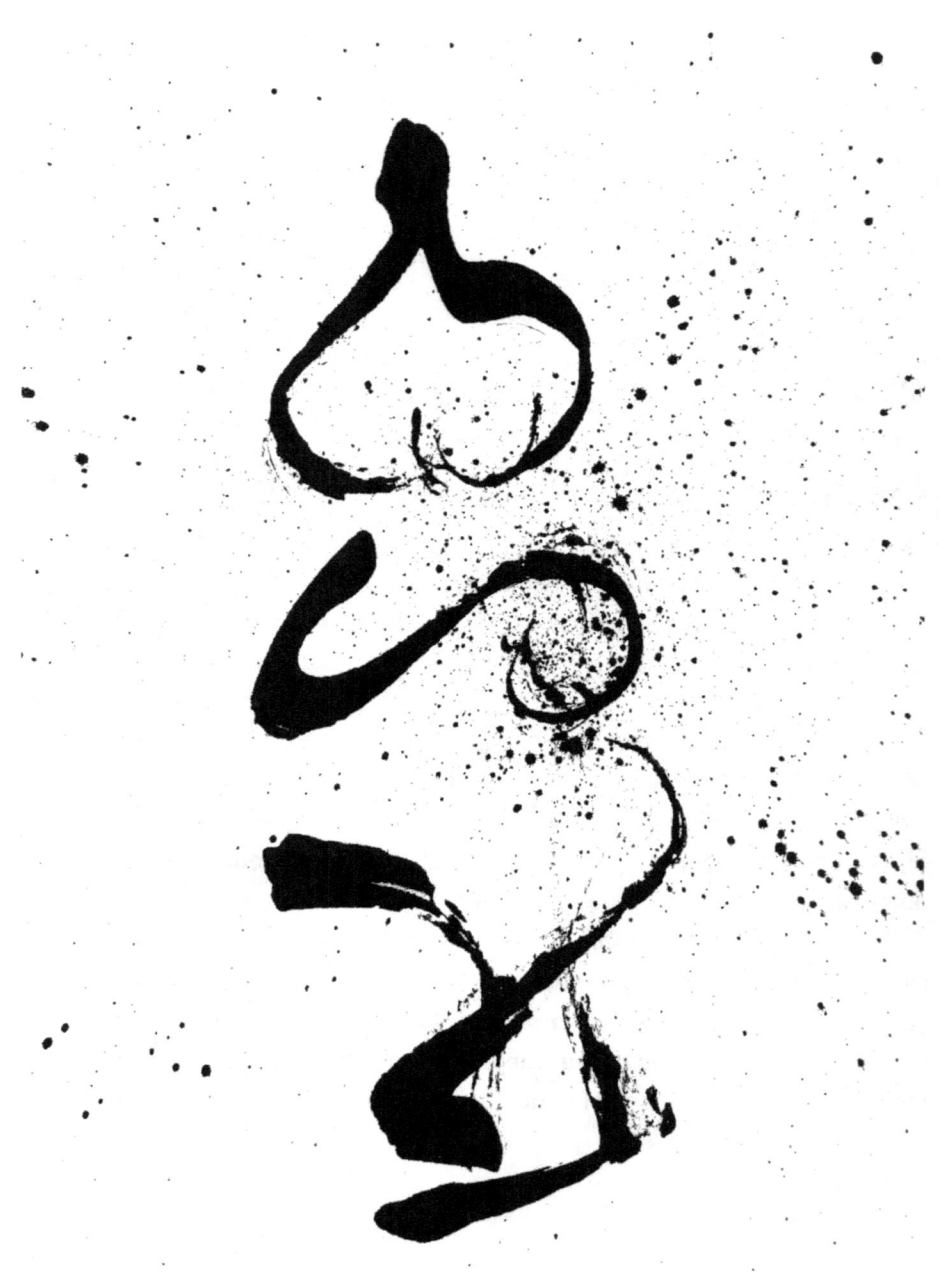

Bahay - Home

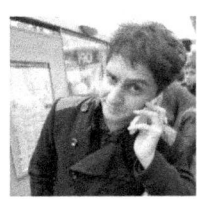

Bobby
London, UK
Facebook: bobstarsky

Being half Filipino & half English, growing up I had trouble figuring out my identity while growing up. I'm British yet was raised within the Filipino community. But a number of times I was told I'm not a true Filipino, whether it be because of the color of my skin, the fact that I can't speak any Filipino language, or even because my nose is pointed. It was difficult growing up when some do not view you as an equal for reasons I now find to be ridiculous. But despite the ignorance of some, I found my home. I do not mean home as in the house you live in. There's a saying,"Home is where the heart is." I think that is best used here. It was within the Filipino community I found myself, through friends I made and hold dear to me. They showed me that being Filipino did not mean how pure your blood is or how well you can converse in the native language. Being Filipino is about being part of a community, and I believe a true Filipino does not judge, they welcome and teach. Being Filipino is my home.

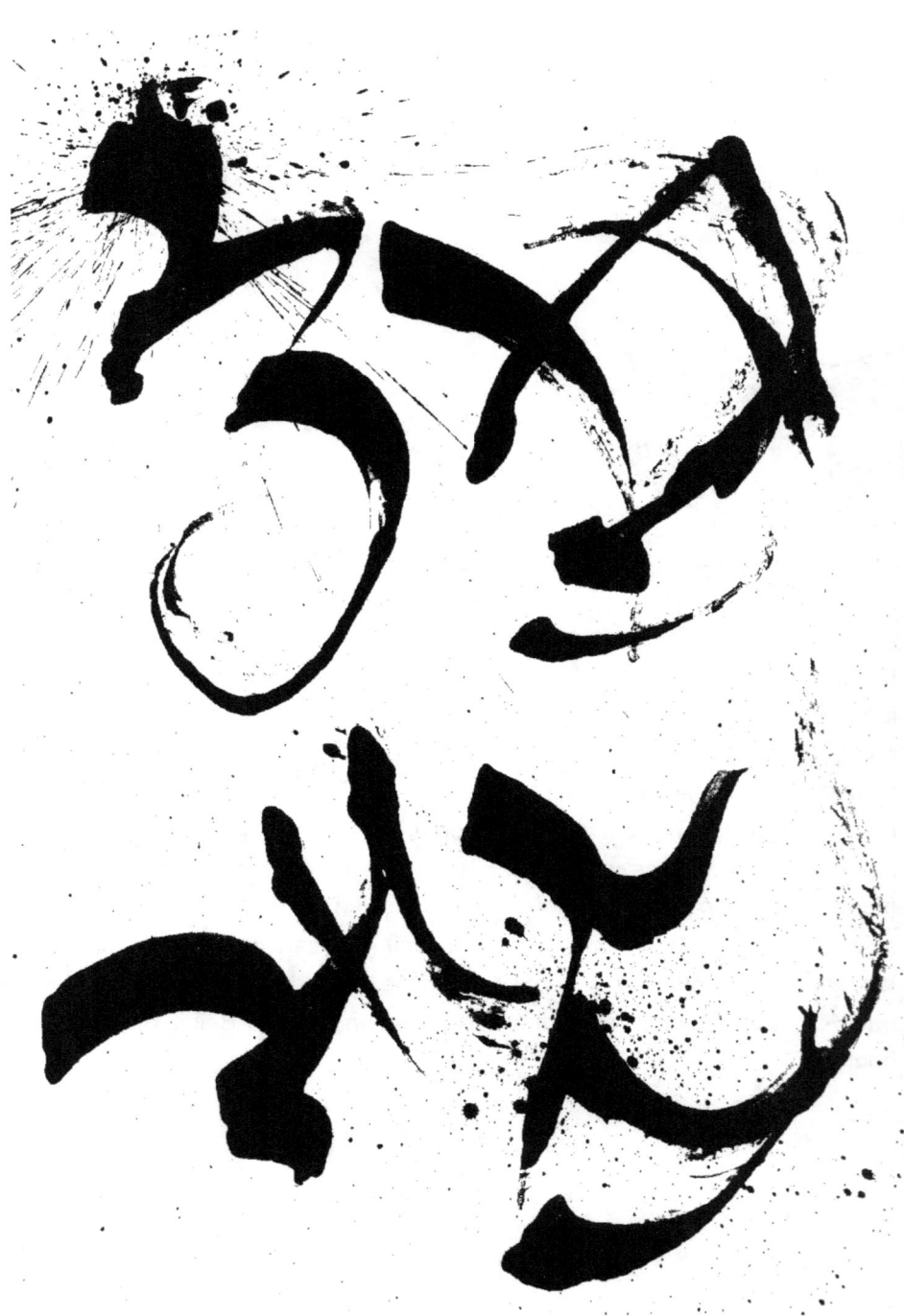

Umpad

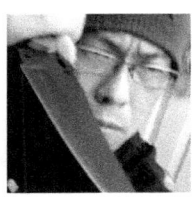

Kibo
Washington, D.C., USA

My teacher Sonny Umpad was a Visayan *Eskrimador*. Out of all the teachers I had in Martial Arts growing up in San Francisco Bay Area, he was kindest and most humble but with great skills. He was a great dancer. I remember how kind he was to and share what he had with his Visayan Eskrima and his teaching. A lot of times he would ask me to go to this new buffet restaurant in Alameda and a Filipino restaurant in that area. He would always want to pay for me. One time, I was going through money problems and he told me to just come and train. How did he give me permission to teach his Visayan Eskrima system in my first year in his class? I came from another Filipino Martial Arts (class?) before I met him. From Villabrille and Largusa Kali. I remember he gave me his card to make copy to use to promote it. He was always a giver. But he's one of the greatest Eskrimador. He used to teach Maestros and Guros. I would see them stop by his apartment and train under him in his living room – a small area, and we would bump into his sofa:) We all called him Sonny! That's way he wanted to be called, not Maestro or Guro. My *kuya*, teacher and good friend. I was 27 in 1997, the year I trained with Sonny. The last thing he gave me was a Handmade Barung sword he made, when I left for the East Coast. He passed away in 2006, of cancer. Now I'm passing it on to my students and in the Philippines. Pugay.

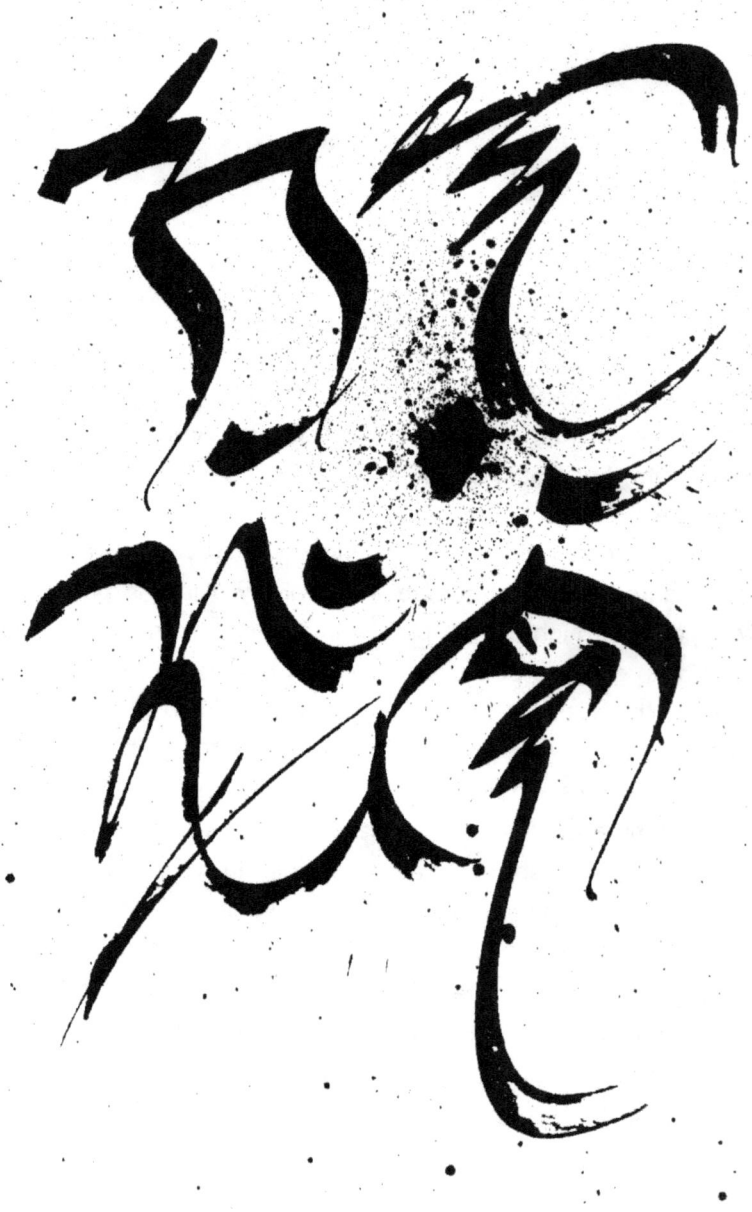

Golondrina

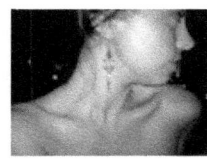

Cristina Rose
Los Angeles, California, USA

La Golondrina Ibon, the river swallow bird, is my guide. She speaks to me about my ancestors, and she teaches me to be more "como pajaritas," like birds, flying and enjoying all that life has to offer. She is a hard-worker too and builds her nests along the rivers, rivers that cross borders and cover the Earth. Putting her efforts into nepantla and babaylan endeavors, she is a Mestiza creatrix. Her erotic and empowered energy transform everything she touches.

Indeed, the women in my family are all like golondrinas. We have been flying from place to place, fleeing systematic violence(s), and seeking a safe and nurturing space to call home on the Earth. This we do even though we have come from beautiful lands.

Yes, my grandmothers came from gorgeous homelands. My Abuela Priscilla is from Golondrinas, New Mexico: sacred and rich land. My Lola Concepcion is from Cebu in the Philippines: waters with riches one cannot even imagine. Yet, both of my grandmothers had their own journey to Los Angeles to find new jobs and new families.

Although they came to Los Angeles to find a new home, I have journeyed and returned, in the past decade, to my grandmothers' homelands. I wanted to remember where I am from and to find a home for myself. Thankfully, I have found a bit of home in the mountains of New Mexico and Spain as well as on the islands around Cebu.

And yet, in the process, too, I have felt lost and divided. How can I have so many homes? And, can there be homes on borderlands and in diaspora? Sadly, I have often felt so far from home while feeling a bit at home in my "motherlands."

It is when I feel so far from home that I am reminded, by the golondrina ibons themselves, that my home is wherever I may be. Yes, I am drawn to the golondrina because she is everywhere. We are everywhere.

When I was a child, I would watch the river swallows fly for hours in the Mora River of Northern New Mexico. They build their clay and sand nests on the walls of the caves, and I enjoyed watching them fly from nest to tree to young to me and back. All the while, the river gurgled and the sunset wind played with us. These golondrinas I also saw around the waters of Cebu and in the Visayan Islands. I saw their spread wings and forked tails around the sacred balete trees. I saw them all around the waters. I saw them dance with the waters and the Earth and the wind and sun.

These golondrinas, and all of the beings I call mothers, teach me and continue to nurture in me a creative and intentional integrity. They show me the way home. They show me I am home.

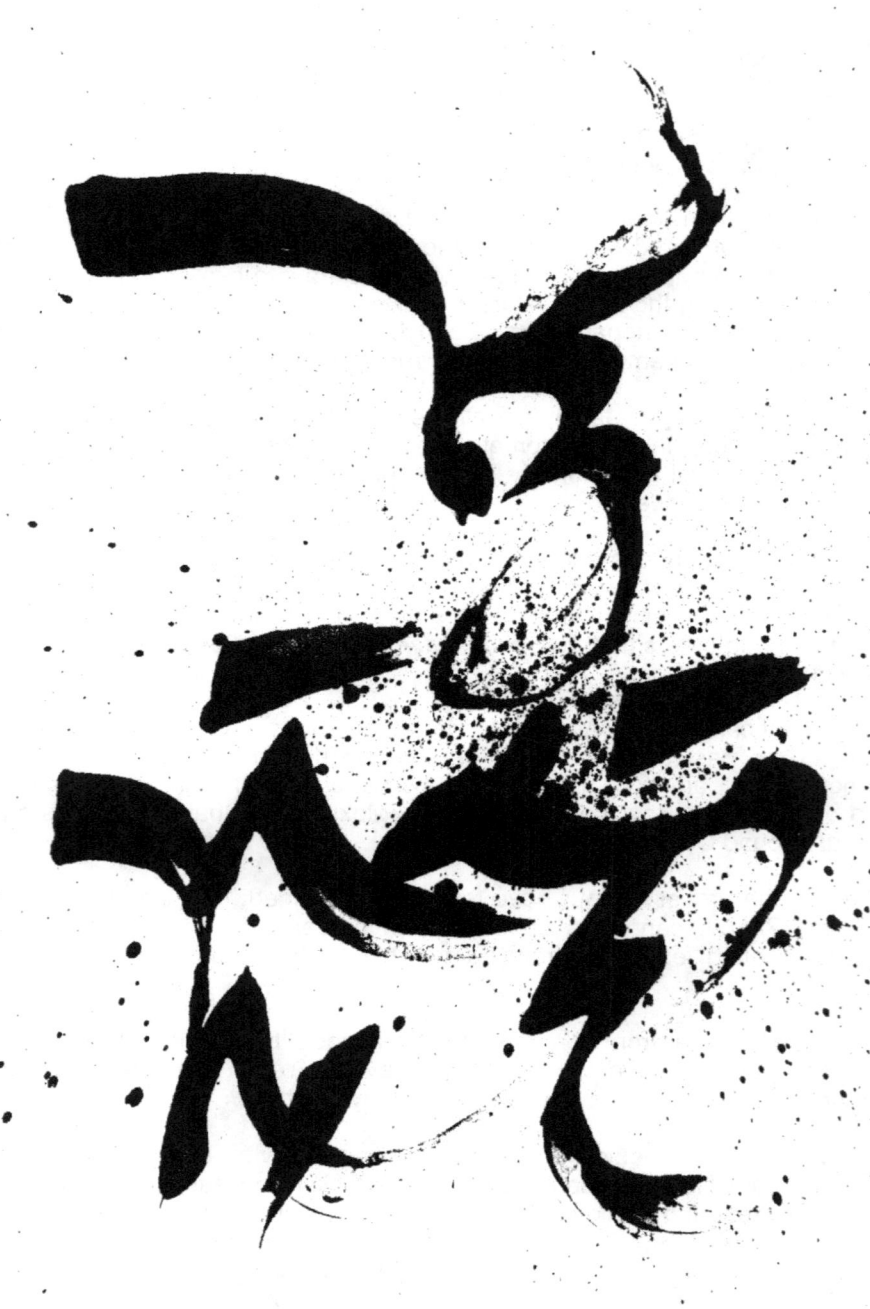

Sarili - Identity

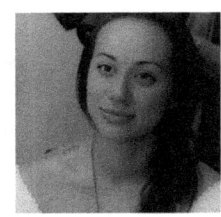

Jacqueline
Edinburgh, Scotland, UK

I don't think I really realized that I looked different until I started primary school and one of the boys in my class called me paki (racist slang, derived from Pakistani).

I was brought up in the Shetland Islands, a small island some 12 hours ferry ride away from the far north coast of Scotland, born to a Filipino mother and a Scottish father.

I always felt challenged at school in Lerwick, Shetland's capital, with the constant pressure to fit in and be liked. I didn't want to be seen to be different and I hadn't ever really acknowledged my Filipino side, and this boy reinforced my thoughts and feelings about not wanting to be different.

The turning point was my first trip to the Philippines with my mum when I was 14. I didn't know anything about the place or people before I went. I couldn't have imagined what it was like, I knew very little about my family there...everything was new to me.

A month of being in the Philippines - seeing, experiencing and understanding and spending time with so much family that I previously knew nothing about - ignited my curiosity about how to be more 'Filipino'.

I started going out to the Philippines as often as I could following that trip. I was fascinated, I wanted to learn Tagalog, learn how to cook, but more than anything I wanted to establish a bond with my family out there.

I learned to embrace my Filipino side and felt a sense of pride to be part of a nation of some of the most hospitable, friendly and loving people I have ever met.

I now have dual nationality. I applied for Filipino nationality last year because I felt it was time to make a claim on what is part of me, and make it more official by having it stated on an official document.

I am still constantly asked where I am from because of my 'exotic' looks, and most people assume that I am Spanish or Latina. But I couldn't be more proud that I am half Filipino and half Scottish, and jump at every opportunity to tell the world. This is who I am and this is my identity!

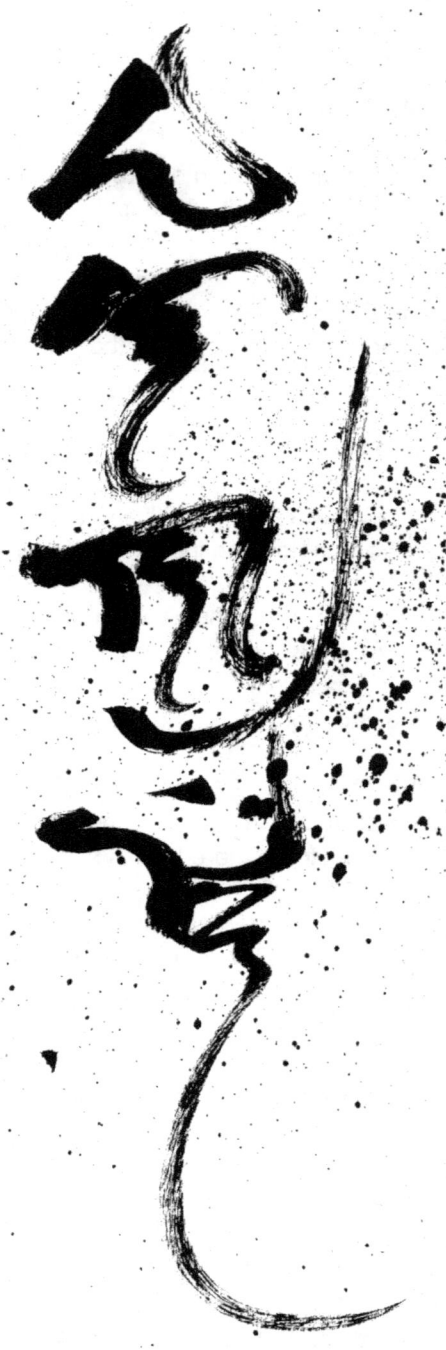

Balanse - Balance

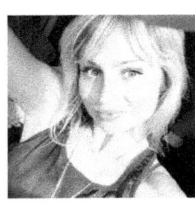

Magdalena
Kwidzyn, Poland

You never know what you can find when you're searching for the unknown. Ever since I can remember, I was always searching for something unique, something I can't really define but once I see it, it takes my breath away. I suppose I can call it a form of beauty...in people, material things, places and ideas. I was on a search for BALANCE. In a hectic life, this word reminds me of the life philosophy and the harmony I want to maintain. For many other reasons I wanted balance to be tattooed on my skin. I spent some time looking at different ideas and there it was. Graffiti? Script? Meaningless lines? I had no clue but I knew that was IT. After contacting the Baybayin website I was fascinated by the origins and history of it and even though I'm from the other side of the planet, it didn't matter. It just felt right. They say with balance comes clarity, but to me it was much more than that.

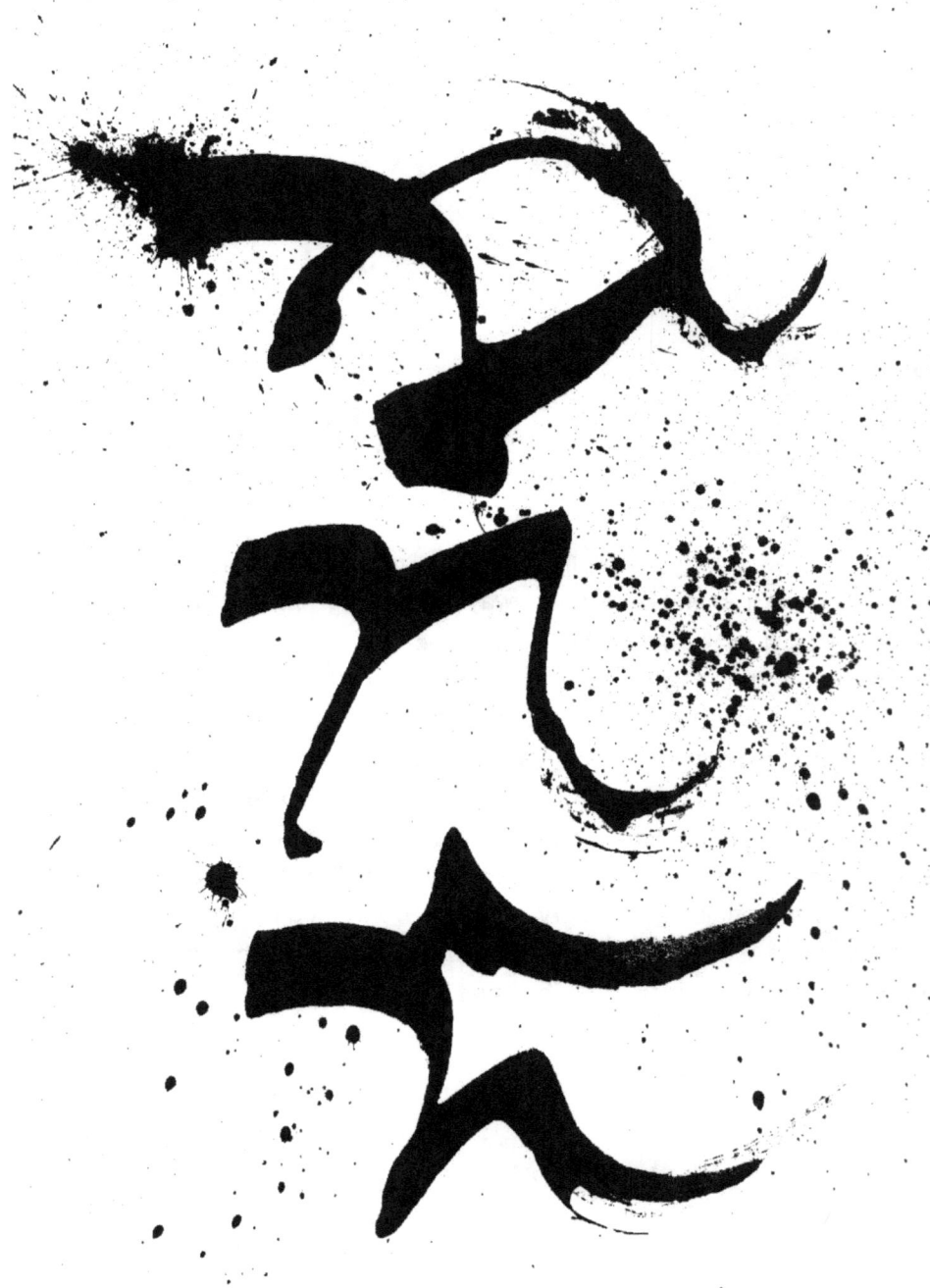

Maganda - Beautiful

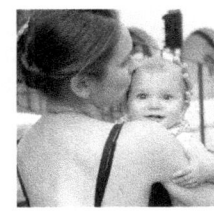

Claire
Oakland, California, USA
Clairemeyler.com

Maganda. Beautiful. It's one of the few words I know in Tagalog. As a fair skinned half-white/half-Filipina kid, adults indulged me when I asked them to speak English. I wish I could time-travel, make that bratty kid pay attention, make meaning out of the words so that I am not struggling to learn it now. Instead, I used to let the Tagalog flow over my ears like music. But I knew when my Titas were calling me beautiful.

When I was pregnant with my daughter, I struggled to find a name that could reclaim the only heritage that I have a deep connection to: my distant European roots aren't alive for me like my Nanay's adobo and lumpia. I want my daughter to take pride in that heritage, too: starting with her name. But I didn't want a name that was too Spanish, so I settled on a word from Tagalog: Maganda. I like that it denotes a goodness or loveliness deeper than surface beauty.

Every time I call her name, I tell my girl she is beautiful. As she grows into her name each day, I laugh and cry at all the trouble waiting for us. Talaga Maganda, my little "Ganda."

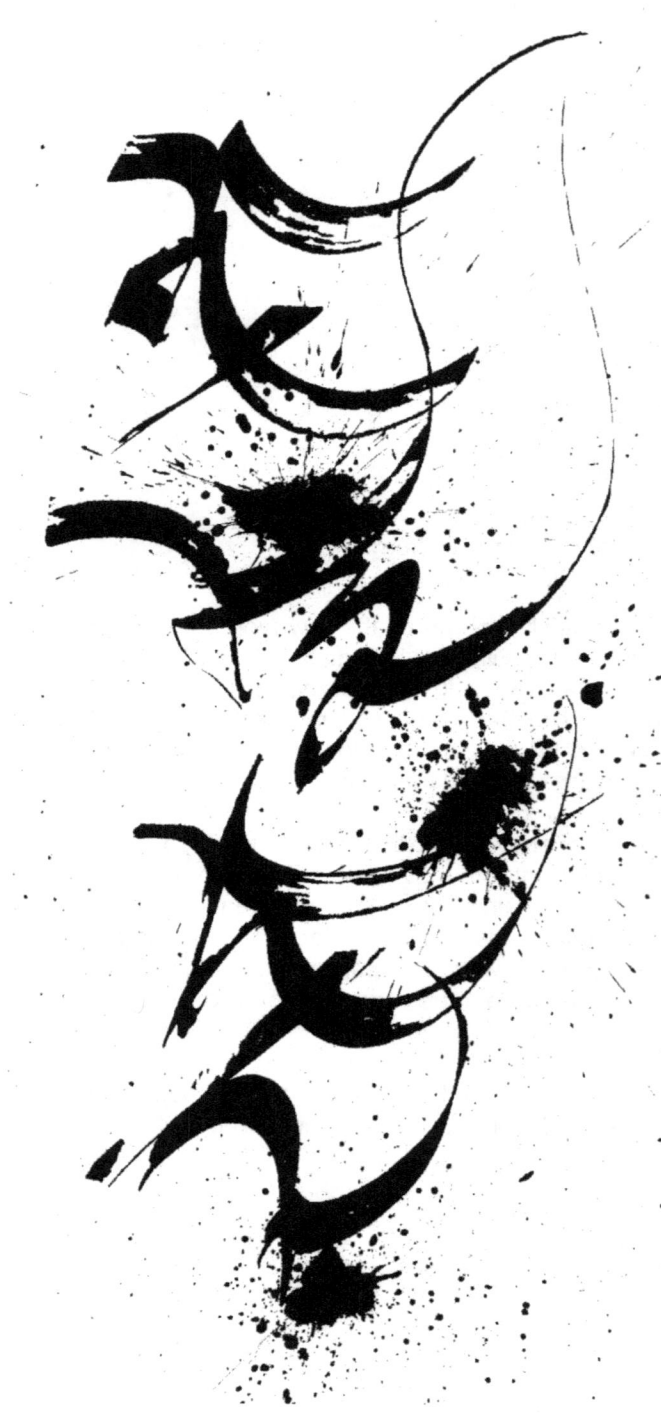

Rosario

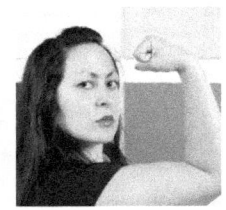

Mari
San Francisco, California, USA

Journey... Process... Resistance... Survival... Organizing... Healing...

This journey has began thousands of years before I was born...
It began with my creator and the world that was created for our ancestors,
but my spirit was born during a time of war... and resistance...
Spaniards killing, raping, colonizing, & christianizing...
My ancestors resisting, surviving, organizing, and fighting
Their symbols of oppression,
transform into symbols of oppression.
One Rosario... saved my family...
Their journey of marching to that inglesia with Rosarios in hand...
Except one... One forgot to bring that Rosario...
So now we are marching back through the battlefield to grab that Rosario...
So we can pray...
Pray for the day that our land will no colonizers.
Pray for our fallen ancestors and their journey into the afterlife.
Pray for our future generations so that they will continue in our
spirit of resistance.
So now we are all marching with Rosarios in hand when we reach the
ingelsia...
Our mouths fall down and our hearts grieve...
that inglesia...
is in ashes.
The same conquistadors who built it have just killed our people who
were inside it.
So then we get to live to create, thrive, and resist...
to tell the story about that one ancestor...
who forgot that Rosario...
because...
One can start a movement...
One can spark a revolution...
One can resist & survive oppression and then live to tell the stories...
and those stories carry on through me.
light candles and pray in the church ruins.

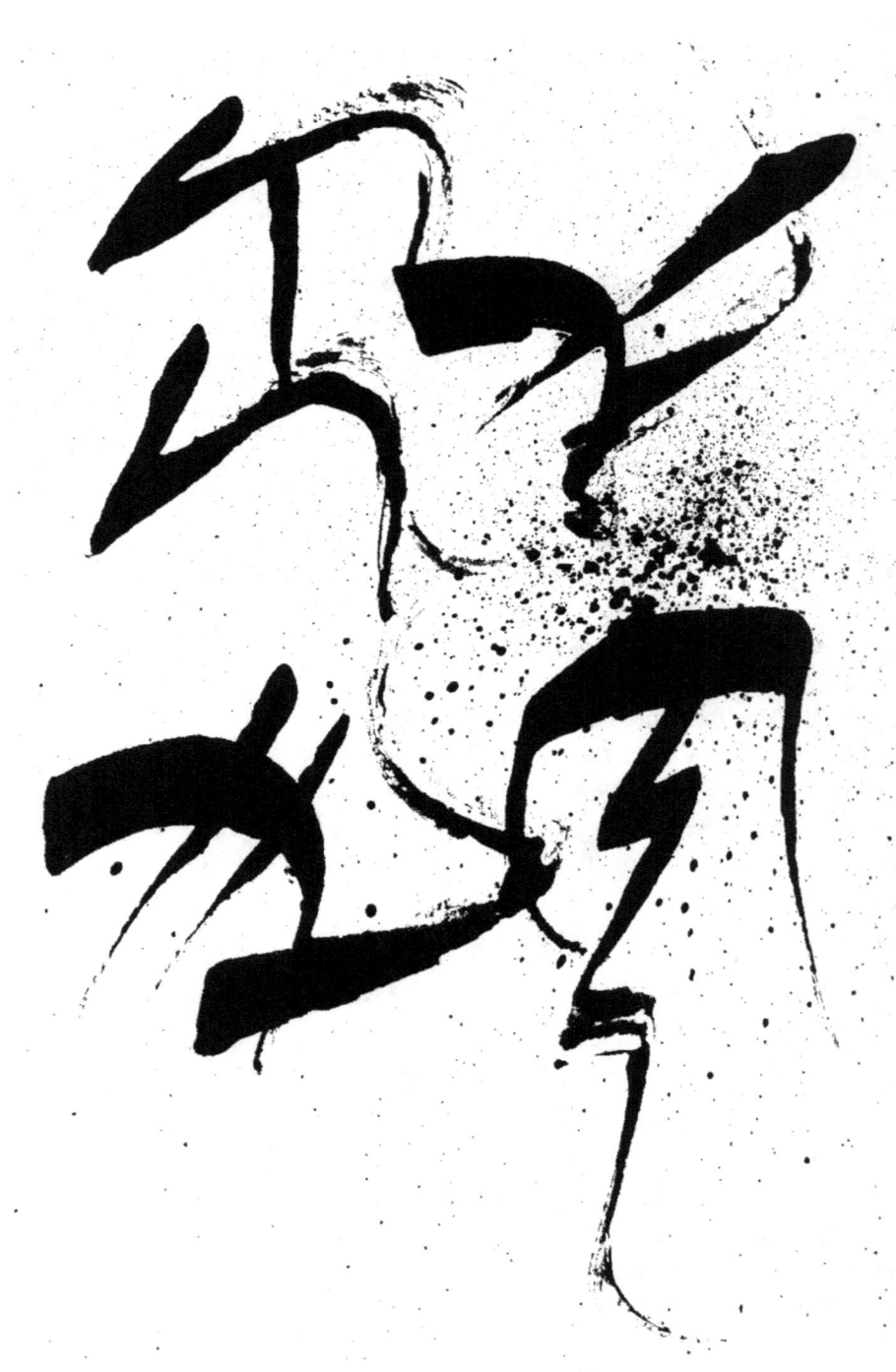

Kamaganak - Relatives

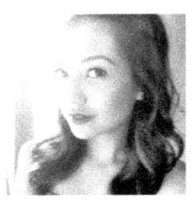

Madel
Sydney, New South Wales, Australia
Instagram: maddiiie__

I was never a "family orientated" type of person until I realized just how important they are to me. I was that person that would skip a family birthday party and be with friends instead. My parents and I used to argue a lot because I was hardly home and I would rebel, still go out anyway, and lie to them. I always thought they were being overprotective, that they just don't want me to be out of the house at all, and never even realized that they were just being parents, worried about me. It got to a point where my extended family got involved. My aunt from overseas, wrote me a letter. She told me, 'friends come and go but family stays together'. I disregarded it after reading it and thought to myself that it's impossible to lose someone or people you've known for a long period of time. But it is true, friends will only be your 'friend' when they need something and you will then know which people are worth keeping when they stick by you. Those times when I've needed help or had a problem, I would always run back to my own family. They were always there for me. You may think this is just one of those typical family stories you hear everyday, but to me it was an experience I learned from.

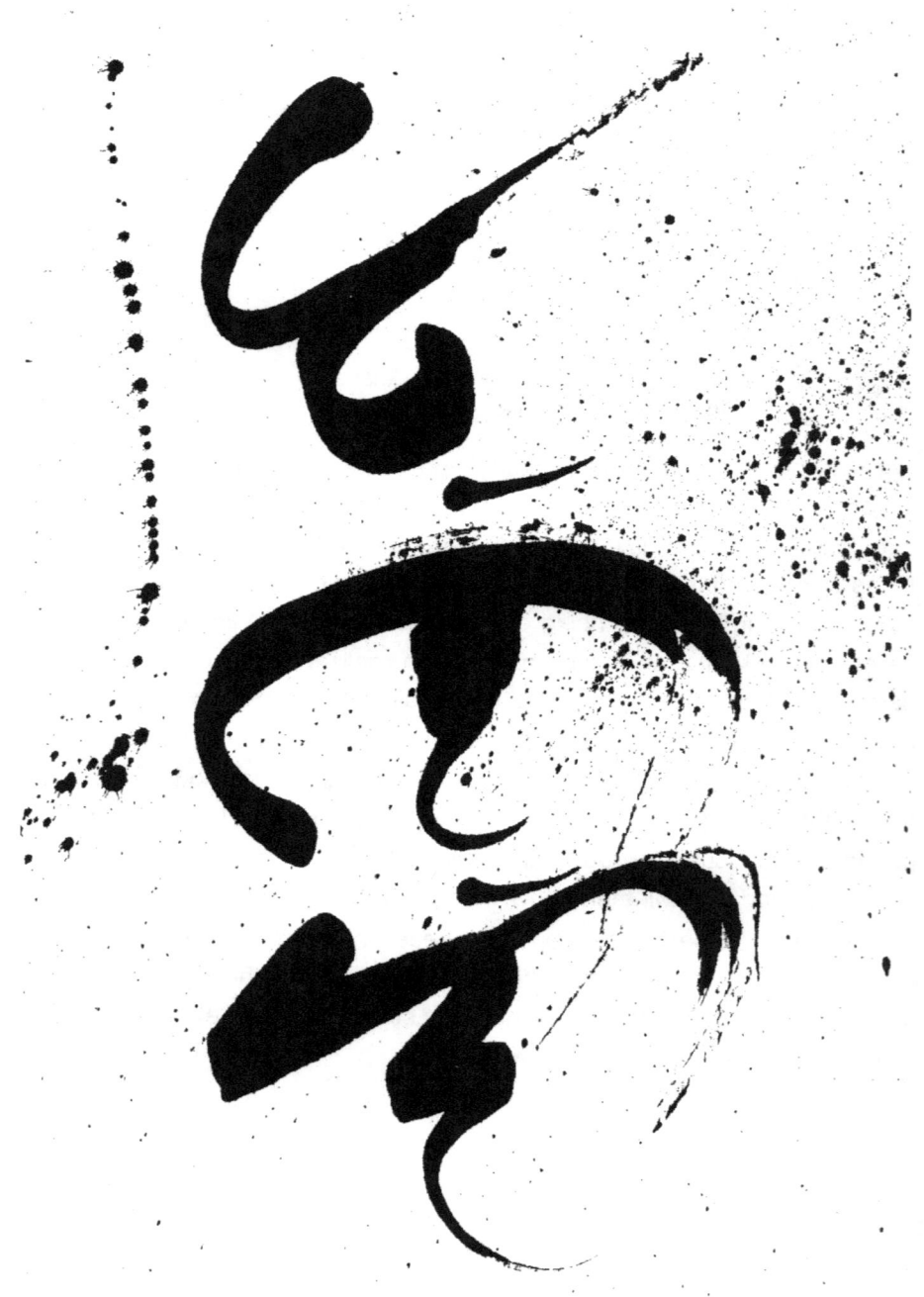

Tekniqlingz

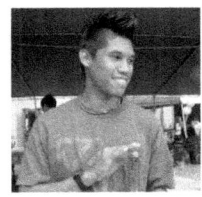

Gabriel
Aiea, Hawaii, USA

I choose the word "Tekniqlingz" because it is the traditional and modern Philippine dance group that I found and direct in Hawaii. If you are Filipino, you are probably saying to yourself what? Not techniqlings, it's tinikling! Here is the answer: Technique + lingz = Tekniqlingz. [tek-neek-lingz] Here is our group description: The Tekniqlingz Crew came about through the Tinikling Workshops held by the Katipunan Club of the University of Hawaii at Manoa. They are a traditional and modern Philippine folk dance group which perpetuates the Filipino American youth culture through the creative arts and entertainment. With its foundation based on modernizing traditional Philippine folk dances, the Tekniqlingz are a dance crew in the making which seeks to inspire and influence new innovations to the world of hip-hop and dance. In 2008, when I was President of a Flilpino club at the University of Hawaii at Manoa called Katipunan, I put out some Philippine and HipHop dance workshops not only for the club but for the community as well. When we started performing, it was supposed to be experimental and temporary at first but eventually the community wanted to see more and since then I just flowed with it, continually dancing and performing. I feel that the group is unique like no other and the name consists of two elements which perpetuates art and culture, through traditional and modern elements. We are infamously known for modernizing the most popular Philippine folk dance "Tinikling," to try to make our culture more aware through inspiration and influential means to the younger generation. When we perform for our older generation, we would to show them that we are not tarnishing culture by fusing it, but we are really trying to uplift it and show how creative and innovative our heritage can be! If anything I feel that most of our most appreciative audiences are within the older generation. I guess that makes sense because I think they are the ones that are really understanding the message through the performance. Now I know that there can be criticism and prejudice with the thought that we are just your typical modern Filipino hiphop dance group but that is wrong. We are all about promoting and perpetuating the culture and we also do traditional Philippine folk dances to back it up. When we perform to the youth and younger generation, sometimes the message might not hit them right away. Today's generation might not be able to "get it" right away because of mainstream influences and distractions. Sometimes they might cater more to what is "in" today through American pop culture and the media. When we perform, my personal focus is on the younger generation because they are the future perpetuators of our culture so it's important that they see at least one symbolic thing our of our performance other than the music and the moves. So going back to the name, "Tekniqlingz," it all sums up to putting technique to the tinikling, expressing art and culture that flows with every move.

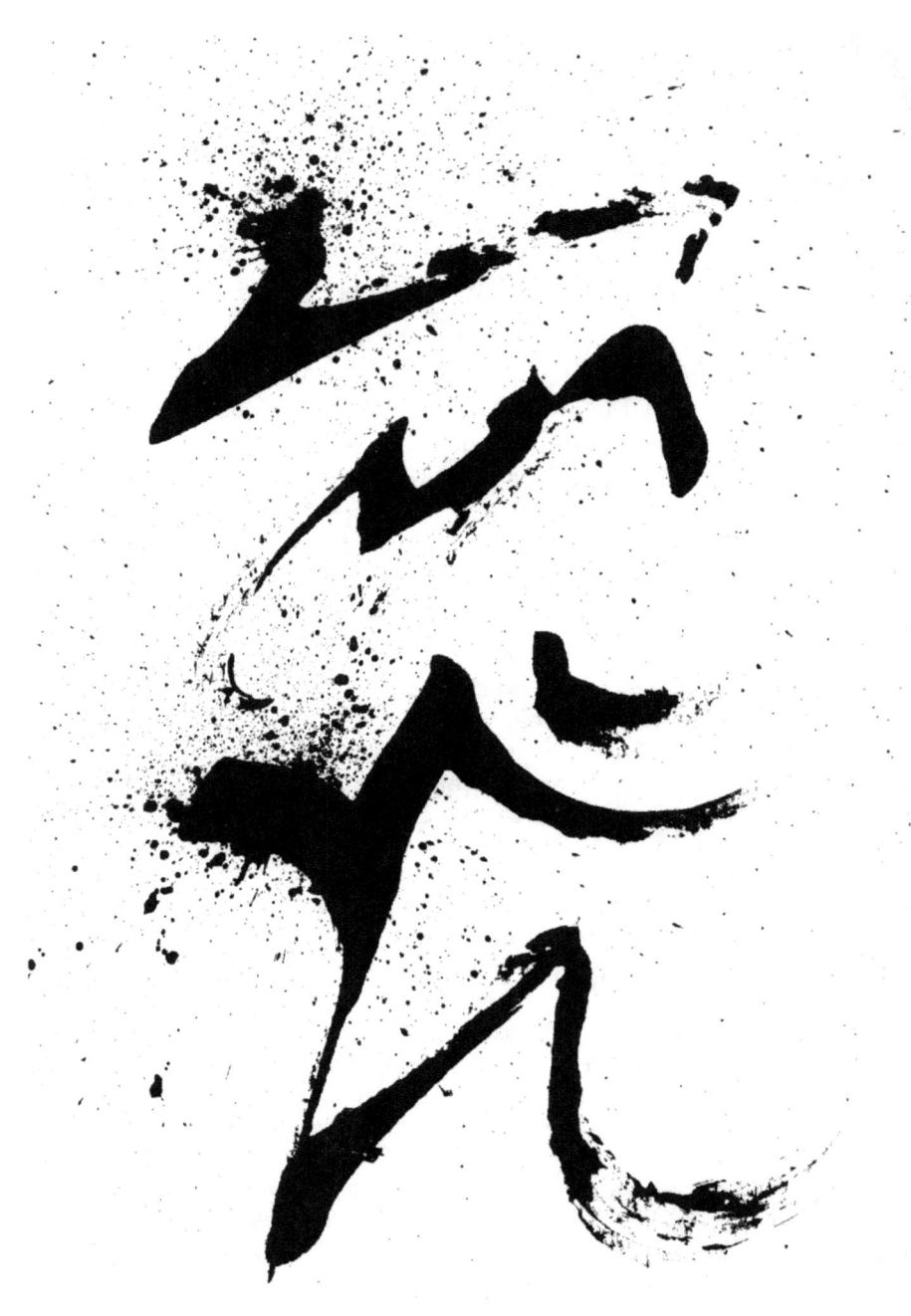

Edith

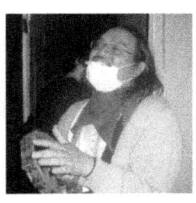

Asher
Spriing Valley, New York, USA

Today, Randall Mann is Teacher on Twitter, not Randal Jacobs (who is too busy channeling flower arrangements in Harlem), although I already miss him, too. Tomorrow, I'd have relearned loss in a custom-made see-through collar, coated in silver. Yesterday, my tomboy cousin Leslie caressed our corpse farewell. Twice forbidden because not only does she leave wildfires in her wake like a Nephilim Siren on weekends, but Auntie Bette transmigrated from Jersey to Sodom for their Wedding Banquet: The Year 7107 Islands came undone. Arvin, my Gay cousin in China, was not in attendance, as far as serpentine vision underwater is concerned. We call her Edith, when homesick, pronounced Edit, after The Flood. AKA Disarming Children of Lot. Date of death. Unknowable.

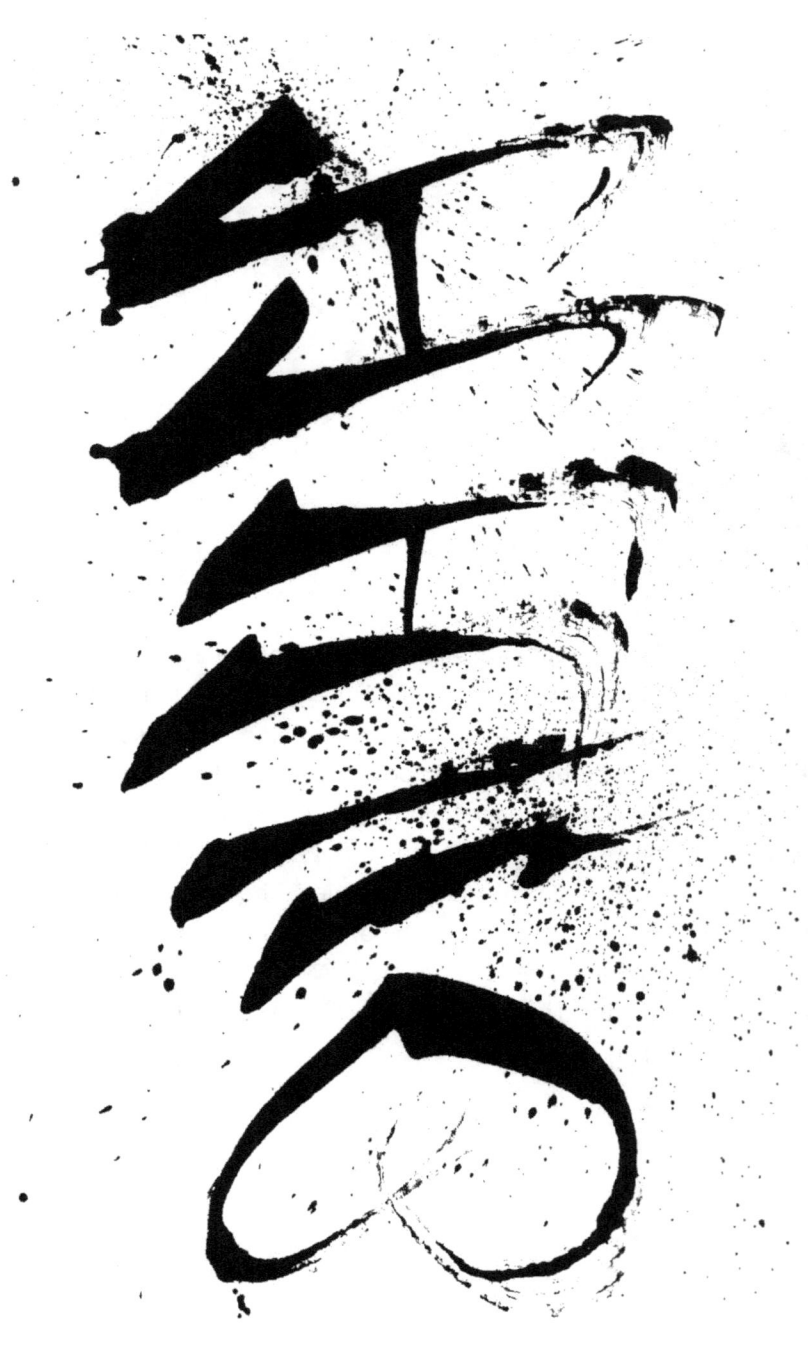

Kakaiba - Unique

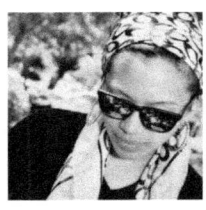

Jho
Vallejo, California, USA
Instagram: jvisualsz

Sometimes its sad to be alone, but it also feels strong to be alone, I am unique and so is everyone else. I like to be the only person in the crowd who doesn't necessarily feel the need to blend in. It's empowering knowing that I can be alone and not feel alone. I have my own taste, likes and dislikes; I have a creative and an idealistic mind.

Being myself is (how about when I've felt most free?)the most freedom that I have ever felt. It's a choice that I'm glad I have learned because you can't be true to anybody else unless you're true to yourself. I like to socialize from time to time, but when I wanna be by myself, even traveling by myself, I don't mind. I don't like to follow if it doesn't click right in my mind; I'd rather be alone than follow the wrong crowd. I don't care if I come out weird, I'd rather be unconventional than be like everyone else. To me, that's boring because doing what you love and expressing yourself, is what individualism means to me.

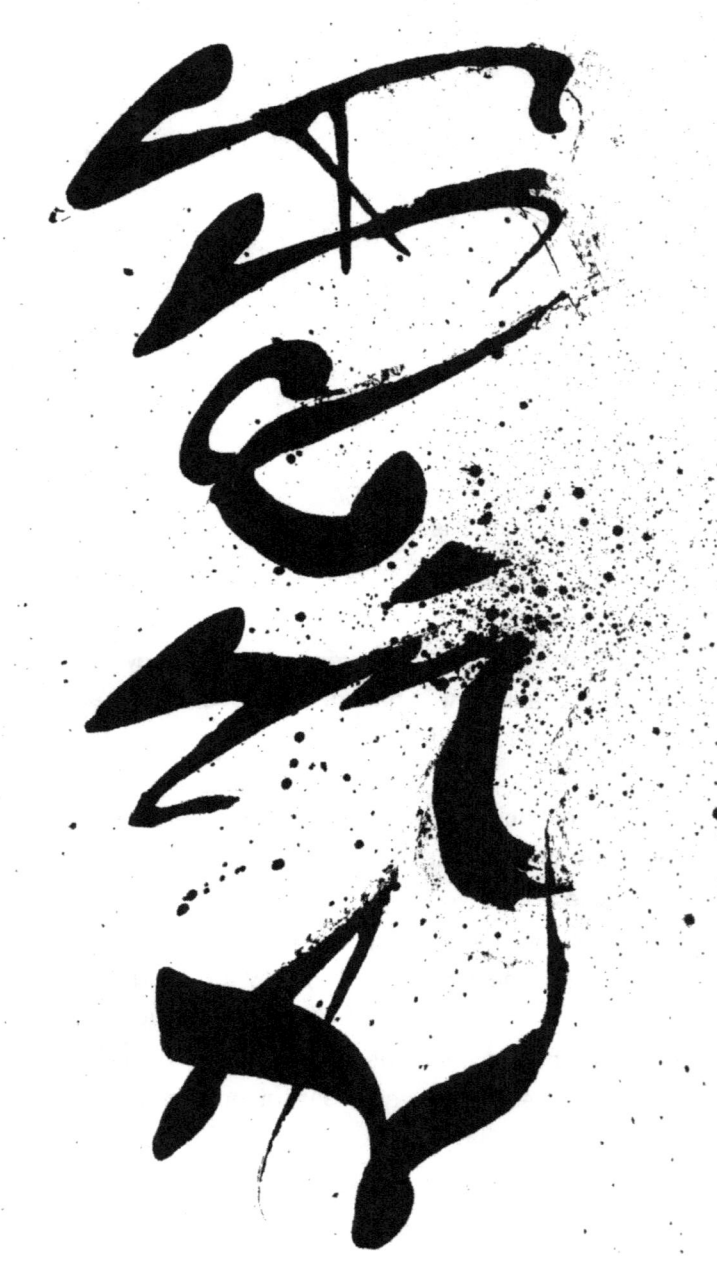

Katangian - Character

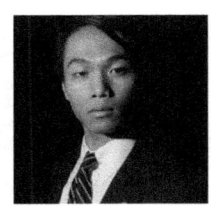

Jacob Ira
Simi Valley, California, USA
Facebook: jacob.ira

Character, how many still have it? Civility, virtue, morals, etiquette, discipline, honor; these are some of the traits that shapes up a humans character. In our latter days, meeting a person with [noble] character has become a rarity and is almost quite impossible to come around. We live in the world now with the human population that simply had forgotten these traits and walks around with no respect whatsoever, even for themselves. Much worse, is that it is highly evident as well with the younger generation. Building a noble character can be a challenging task, but trust me; it is the most notable task one can venture. Self-mastery is the key. I always advice it to people that if you master yourself, you will then master the universe. Self-cultivation or self-growth is an endless process for we humans of imperfections are bound to make mistakes. But that's okay, for from our mistakes we can then learn to shape ourselves to become a better person than we were yesterday. So go on, and examine yourself. Develop and build character that you can be proud of. Character that will echo and will leave a legacy throughout your history and the remaining breathes you have on Earth. "Chisel away the unessential" as Sijo Bruce Lee once said; to reveal the true beauty of the sculptor where your Soul resides in. And while your at it, once you have created and have a great control of your character; be sure to share the qualities you have developed and help another Soul develop theirs. Lastly, to leave you one more piece of advice; leave this world far more better than you have entered it.

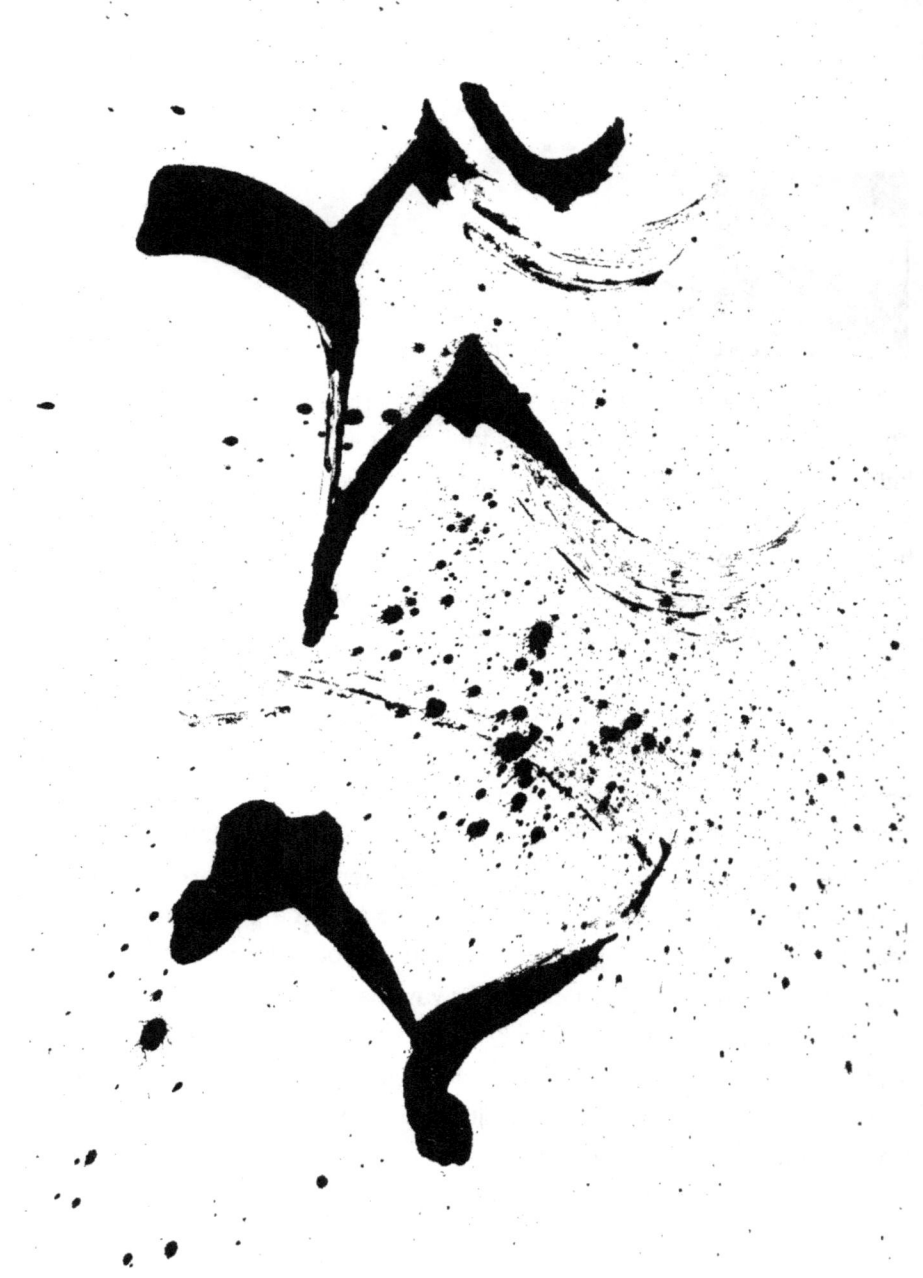

Diwa - Essence

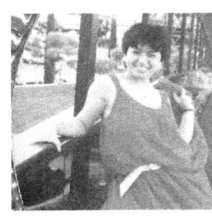

Vilma
Las Vegas, Nevada, USA

Malasin mo Pilipino saan ka man sa mundo,
Hinugot man sa hirap pangarap mo'y inabot mo.
Inang bayan at lahi nag bigay buhay sa iyo,
Pait mong nilisan handog sa mahal mo.
At sa gintong daan na iyong nakamit,
Sa iyong paglalakbay sa masarap na panaginip
Huwag sanang limutin ang diwa na pilit
Upang adhikain ay siyang makamit.

Pilipinos should not lose the essence of who they are in their quest for their dreams and success for their loved ones. Sadly many have lost their identity as Pilipino.

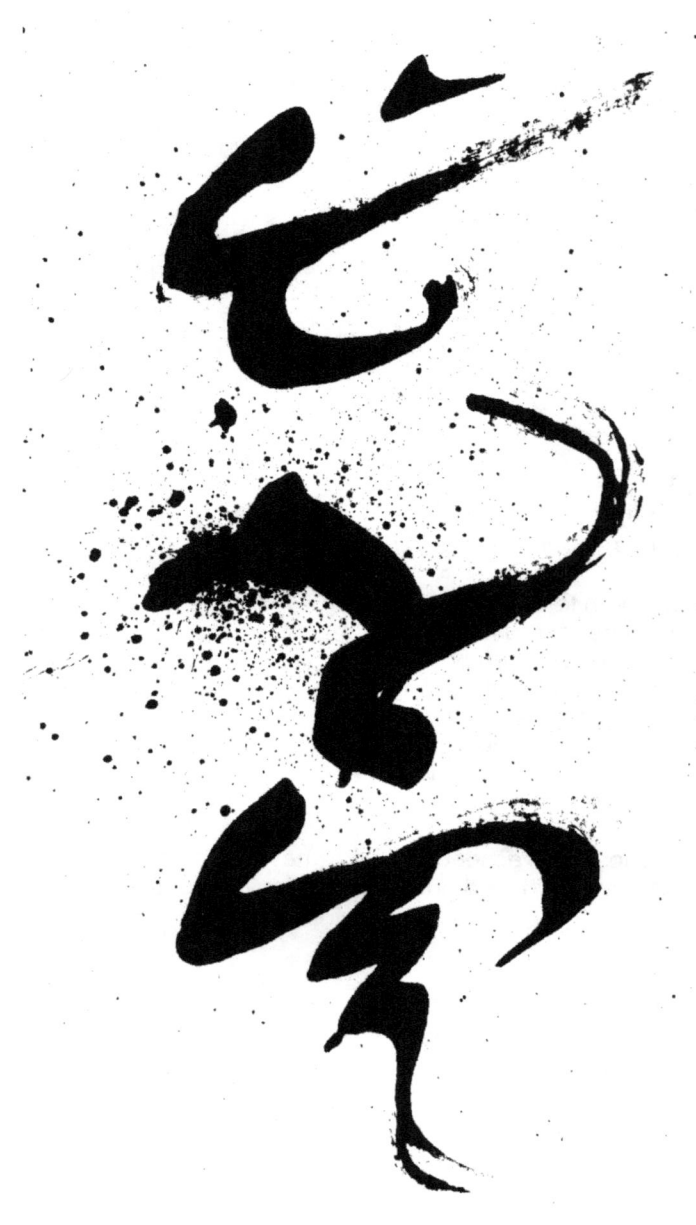

Tiwala - Trust

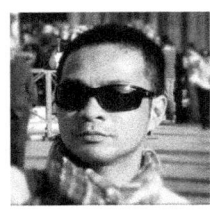

Randy
Wiesbaden, Germany

I trust people easily with no expectation of return, but some abused it. I gave them a second chance & they took it for granted & failed again.

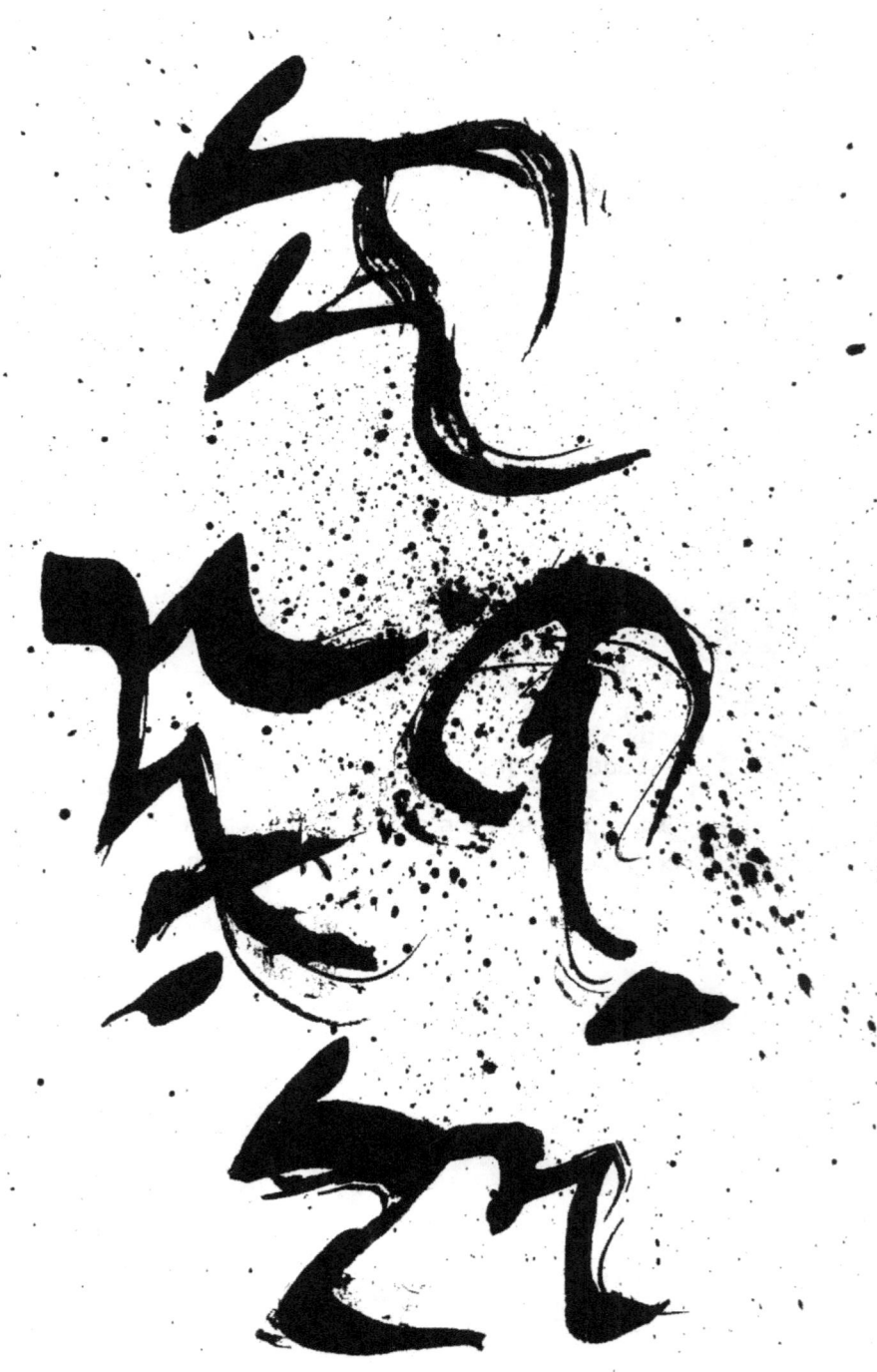

Karunungan - Knowledge

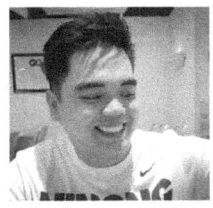

Gab
Quezon City, Philippines

Knowledge is like money: to be of value it must circulate, and in circulating it can increase in quantity and, hopefully, in value.

-Louis L'Amour

Ever since i was a little child being an engineer was always my dream and my goal in life. I wrote on many slumbooks during gradeschool and on my highschool yearbook, that my goal in life is to be an engineer. But fast-forward to after my college graduation: I chose to be a teacher at UP instead of working for big multinational corporations. Even though I still became a licensed engineer and still do engineering work for different projects, the most fulfilling part of my job is sharing what I know to with my students and helping them achieve their goals while serving my country. The opportunity to share my knowledge to with other people was one of the main reasons I chose this career path, and hopefully, someday I can inspire and mentor more students who can contribute to the progress of the Philippines.

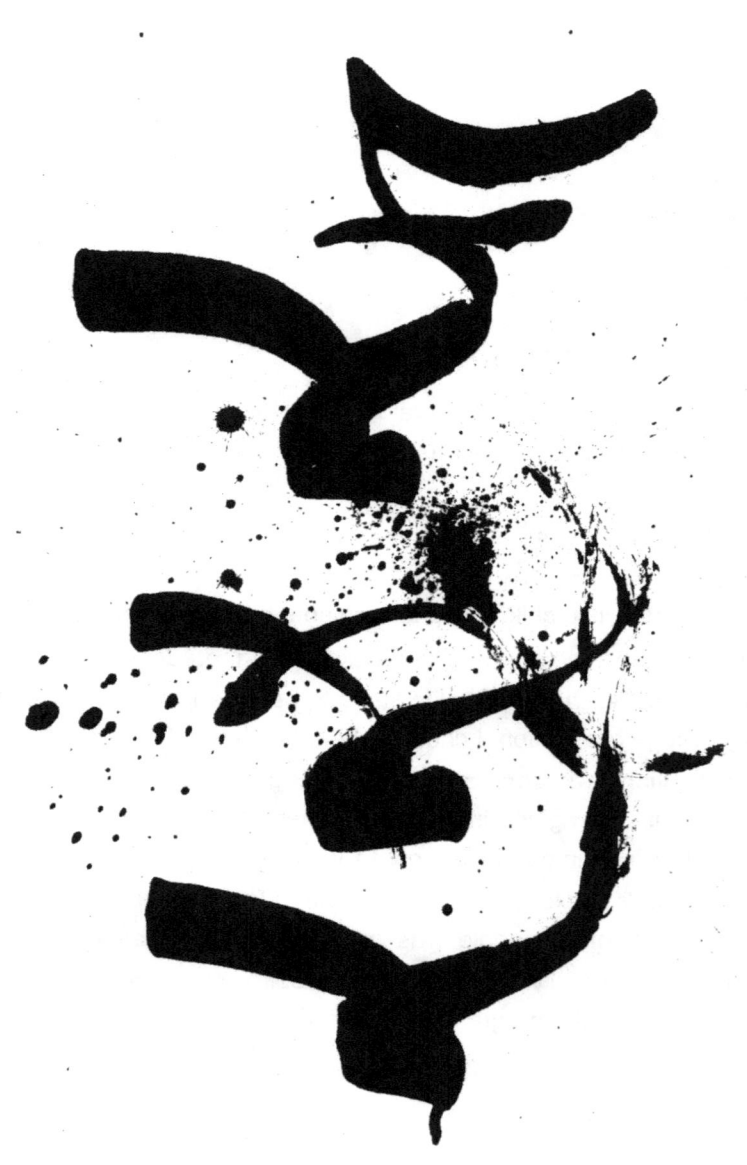

Pamilya - Family

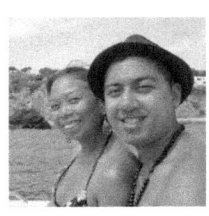

Mae & Adrian
London, UK
PhilippineGenerations.org

For us, the most important thing in our lives is our Family. Our word is 'Pamilya'. Family is one of the most important values in a Filipino household. We both grew up with similar 'Modern Family' experiences, ideals and aspirations, although mine were from London, Mae's were from Philippines. No matter what happens, no matter how non-traditional our family is, our family has always been there for us. All families quarrels and have misunderstandings, but this is put aside during tough times and to help the family progress. Growing up, we both wanted to have our own family and be the best parents we could be to our children. Now that we have our own household and our own family, we are determined to show our kids how important family is in life.

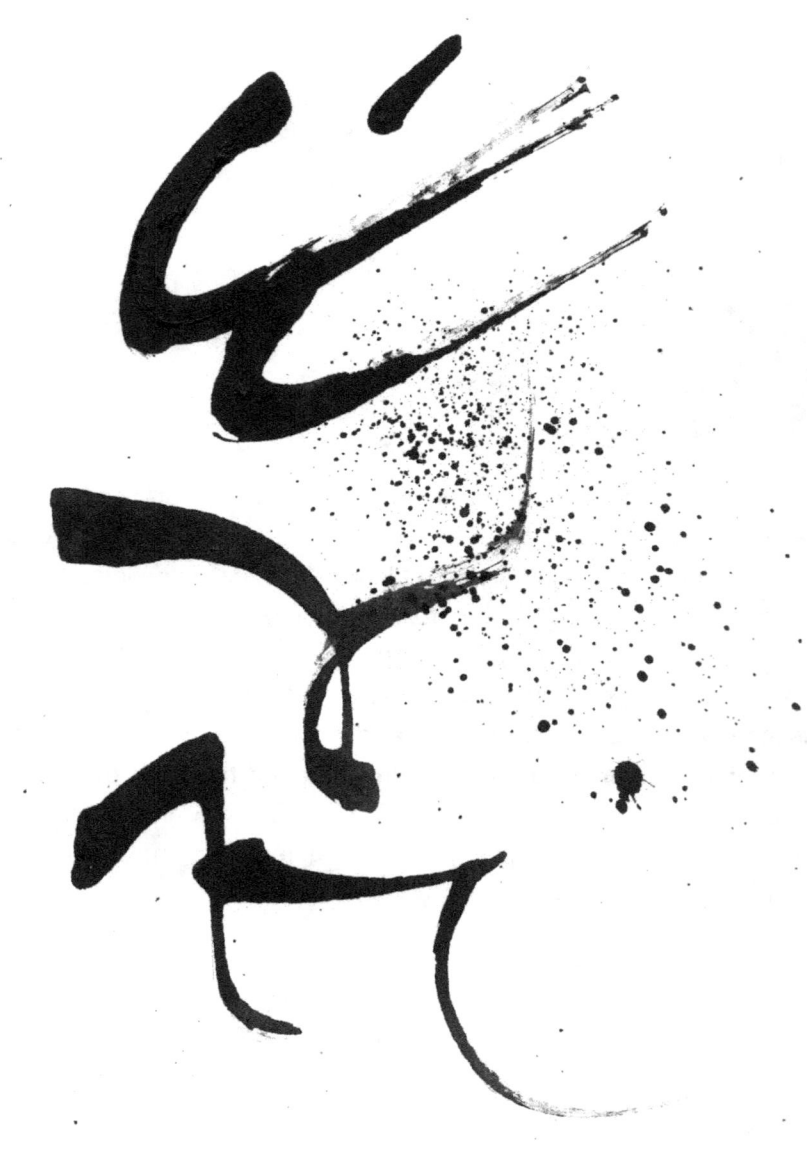

Tiyaga - Perseverance

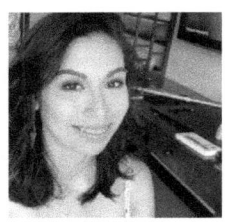

Leah
Winsor, California, USA
Facebook: Barker.Leah

Friends call me as a "fighter." Not a combative hothead but someone persistent. I didn't see it until I thought about how I've turned unexpected challenges into happy accidents simply by persisting.

It started when my mom visited family in Cebu while pregnant. I decided to look at the world too – three months early. I ended up fighting for my life with the help of many Philippine doctors, a few machines and a USAF medevac. The competition of growing up with five brothers nurtured my persistence.

I found my passion in ballet, even though I knew I was too tall and clumsy to make it a career. I stuck with it for fifteen years and loved the challenge. I chose my college for its academic rigor before discovering that the hard part was living on a nearly all-white campus. I took so many anthropology classes to connect to my roots that I accidentally minored in it. After graduating, I accidentally adopted three dogs. Now I love the challenge of training a Pit Bull to run an agility course.

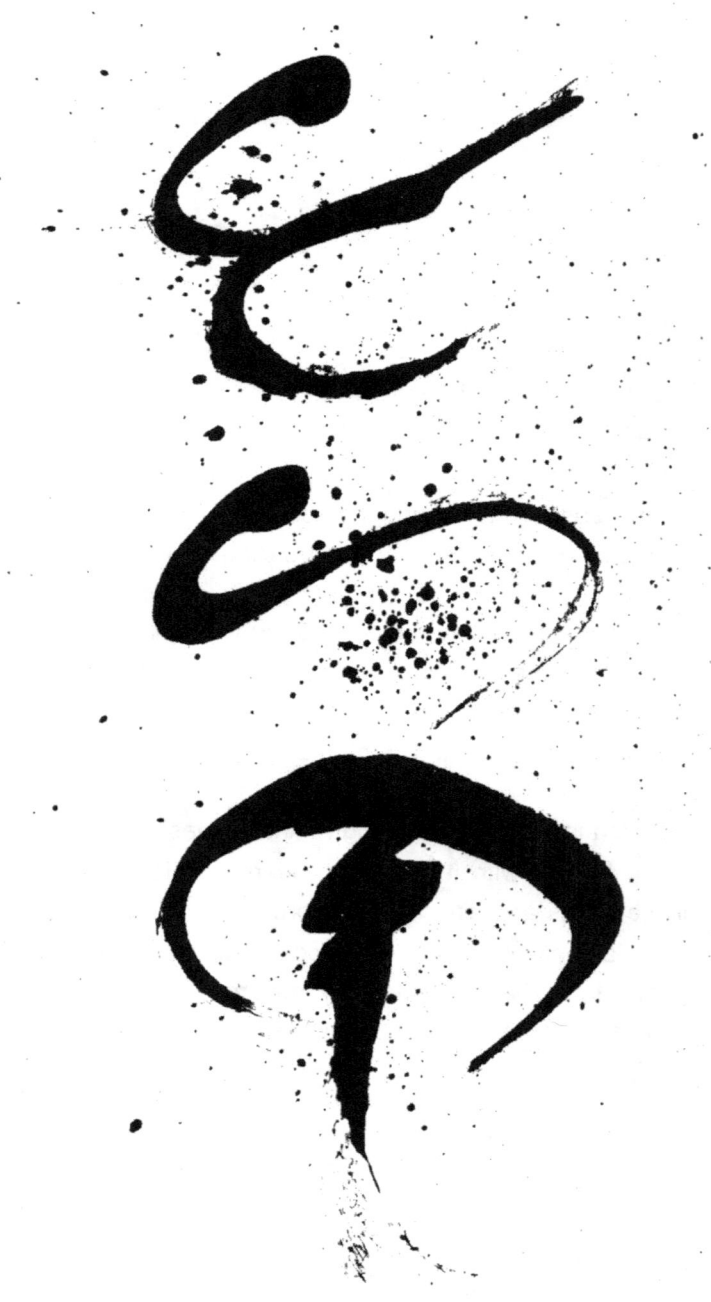

Tadhana - Destiny

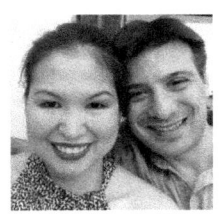

Pinky
Bari, Italy

After modeling in Manila for 10 years, I decided to go back to my hometown of Davao (Philippines) to open up an Italian restaurant at the local mall. I would work everyday from 9AM to 10PM and had no social life. One of my best friends suggested that I try meeting someone online. At first I hesitated because I've heard of all the horror stories of online relationships. I decided to give it a try and see if I can meet with anyone that I chat with about Italian food. This is how I met my future husband. He was in the chatroom hoping to practice his English with someone. We instantly got along and he visited me in Davao a few months later, where he met my family and close friends. A few months later, we were married and I followed to Italy. We've been married for more than 10 years, with 3 kids, and still happily in love. In our opinion (my husband thinks so, too), we were really meant to be. It may sound corny but I believe with all my heart, that I got my happy ending.

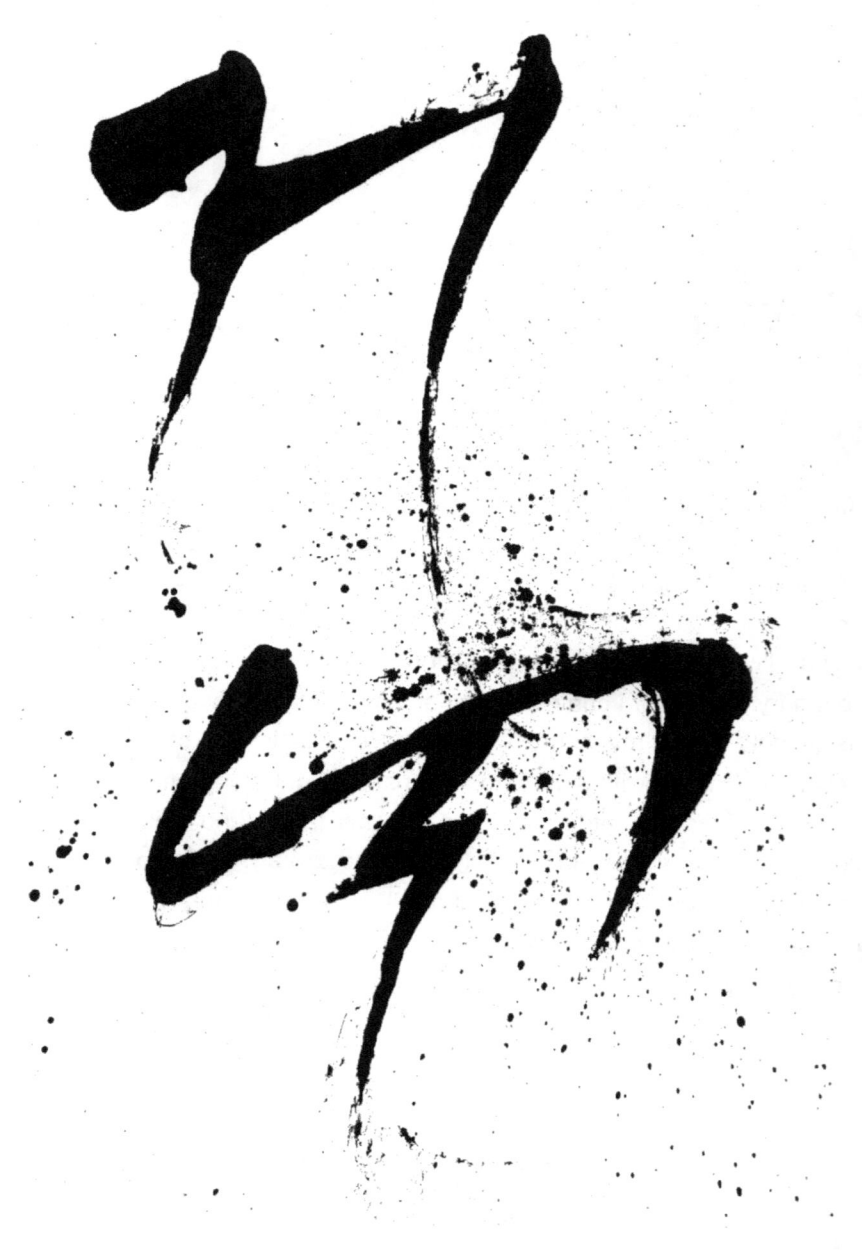

Galang - Respect

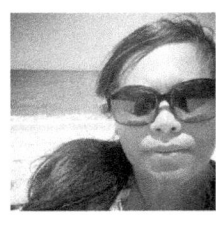

Arlene
Makaha, Hawaii, USA
Behance.net/arlenechiqui29a3

The word Galang to me would be something neither wrong nor right. Each individual has his or her own way of expressing appreciation. In my case, life is about options and MORE options that are nearly seen or tangible. I shape it to my best interest, the magnitude of my needs, the challenges I can accept, the people I love and admire and many more. On the other hand, growing up as a Catholic and had gone to a Catholic School in which Religion was a required class subject, I remembered falling in line out in the hallways with the rest of my classmates during school time. We were all getting ready to walk to the chapel, rehearsing our confessions silently to ourselves, not even knowing what I was truly confessing for, but I listened to my other classmates reciting their confessions. As a result, I did my best to confess my sin(s) to the Father behind the door window. Since then, I explored and have learned a small amount about other religions, such as: Christians, Jehovah Witness, Buddhism, Islam and so on. In retrospect, I learned to respect each unique religion practices.

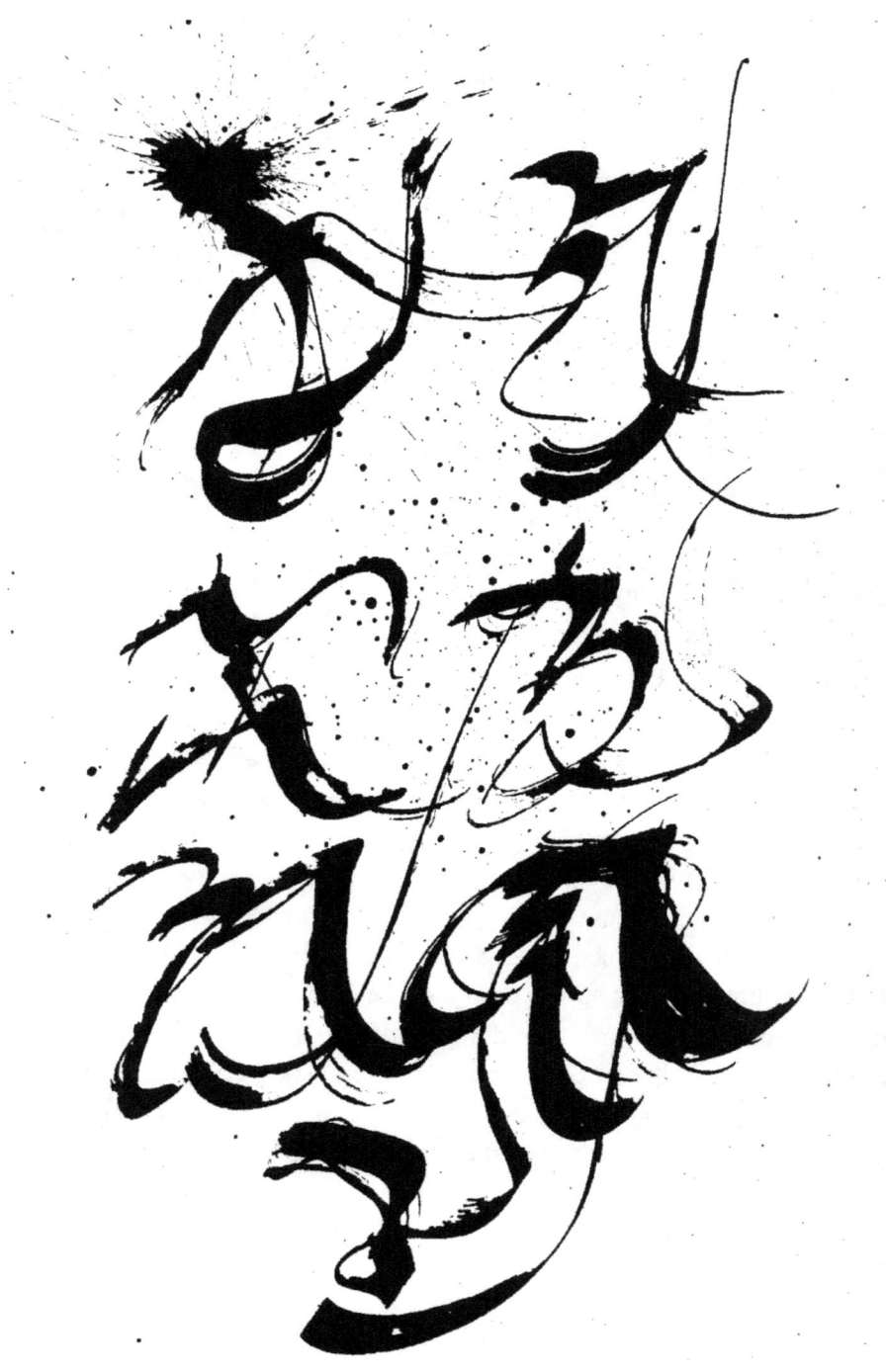

Magkaugnay - Interconnectedness

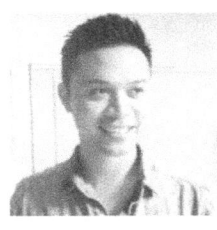

Jed
Los Angeles, California, USA
Kayamanan.org

When I first heard the word magkaugnay, I thought to myself "that's deep!" 11 years ago I joined a Filipino folk arts company where I learned about magkaugnay or interconnectedness. Being born in Cebu and raised in Los Angeles, I thought I had knowledge of Philippine culture because I spoke Tagalog and Visaya. It wasn't until I joined Kayamanan Ng Lahi Philippine folk arts that I learned more. It's about dance, music, and about learning and internalizing the Filipino concepts and being. Magkaugnay to me, is a thoughtful way of explaining life and its constant transitions.

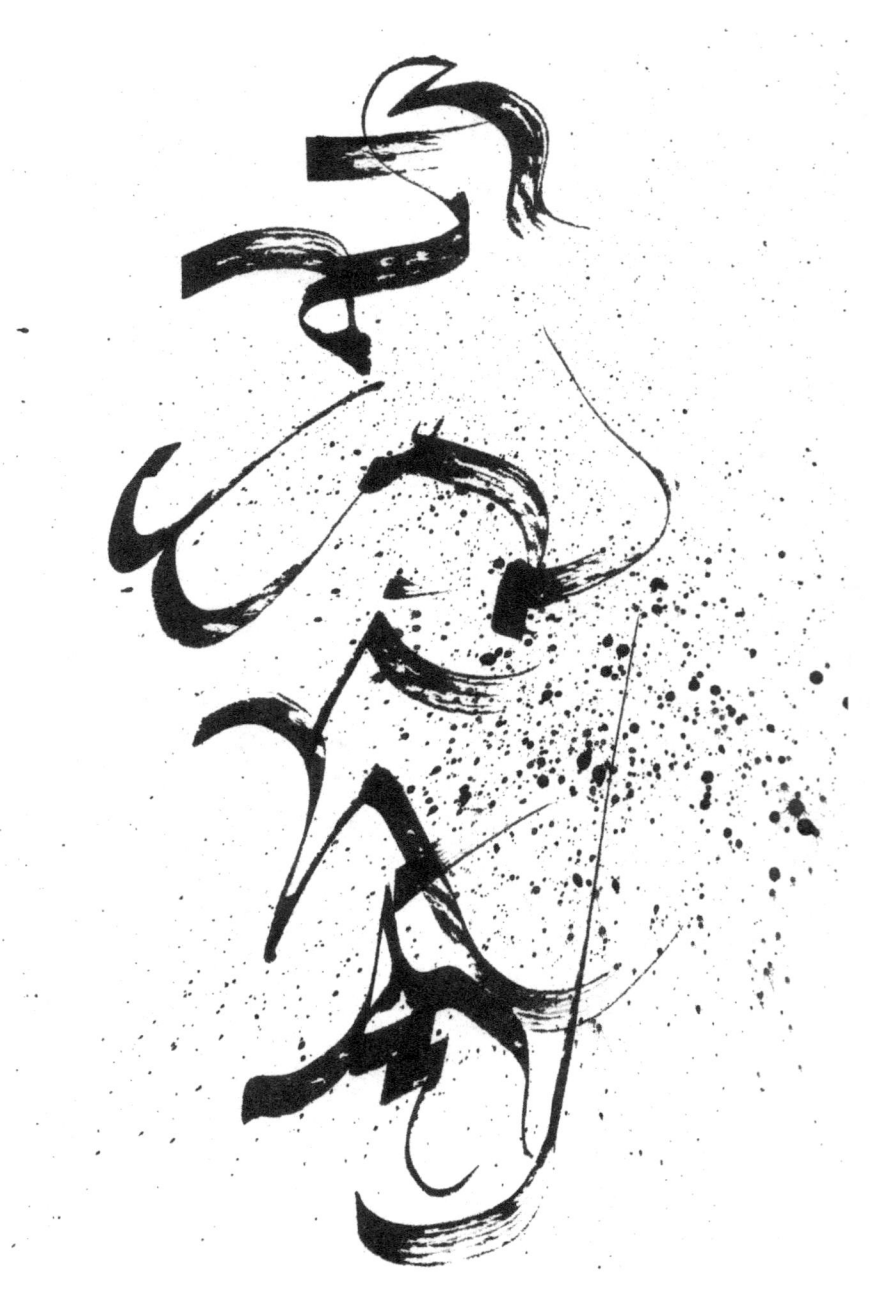

Patawarin - Forgive

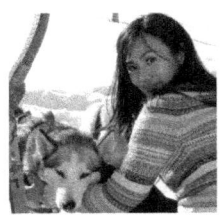

Rossanne
Toronto, Canada

I either heard or read somewhere that forgiving enables healing and growth. It also lets us move on with life. But perhaps I'm a coward because I'm unable to forgive.

One person I have difficulty forgiving is my father. He was abusive and to this day, refuses to acknowledge the pain and trauma he's caused.

The other person I'm unable to forgive is myself. I haven't done anything wrong really but the trauma I've experienced has convinced me that there's something wrong with me and that I deserve a shitty life. Fortunately, I'm slowly unlearning that. I've realized too that I neither caused the violence I've witnessed as a child nor deserve the abuse and neglect I've experienced as an adult.

I've been told that forgiving takes time and that it has to start by forgiving myself. Perhaps sharing this story will help me begin that process.

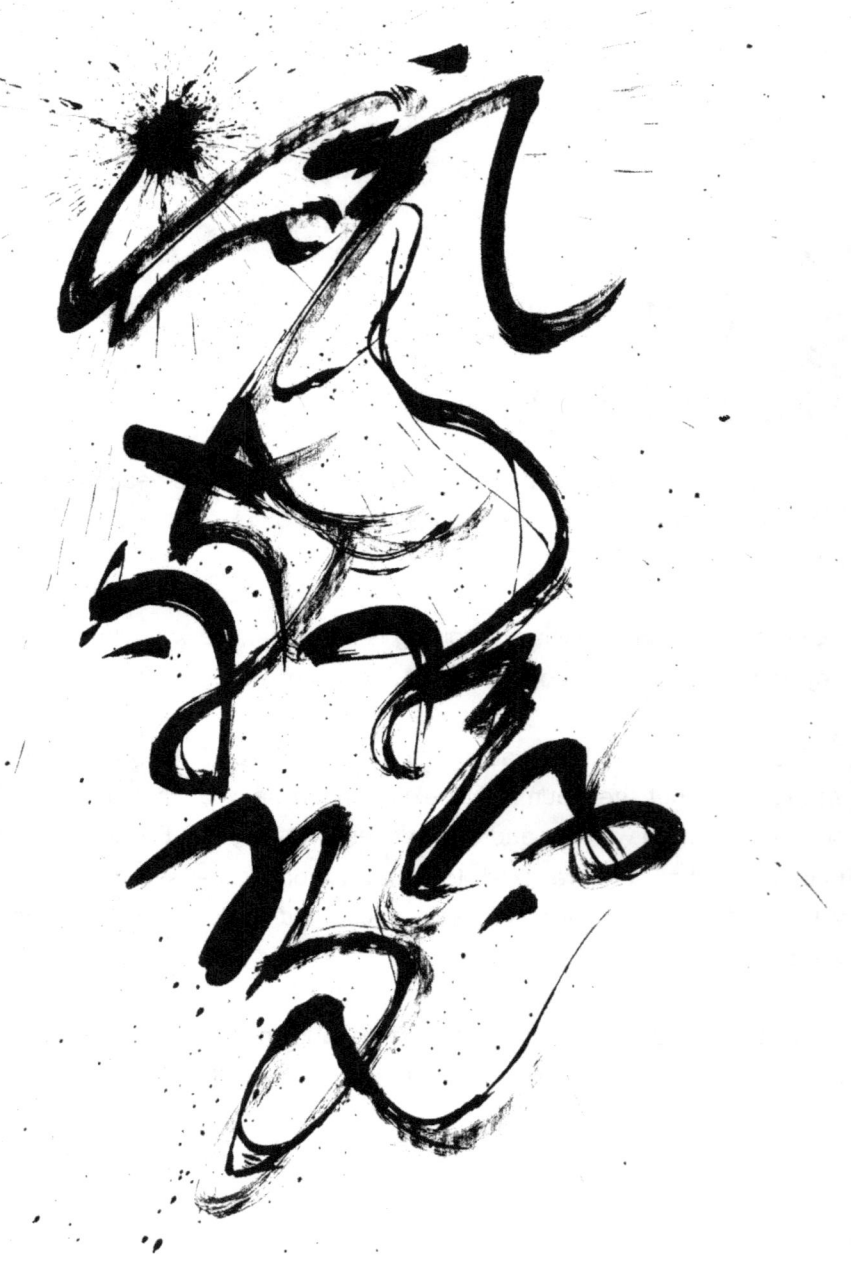

Tagipusuon - Deep hearted

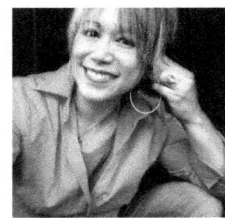

Perla
Austin, Texas, USA
Babaylanmandala.com

I have used the phrase "halin sa tagipusuon" for all my creative works in words & art because it all comes from a deep place within me. it included at the time, the Bahala Na Meditations.

In 2002 a shaman healer or hilot was working on my body full of pains & blocks from my childhood past. she worked around my reclined body & finally came to my belly & pushed into my solar plexus very deeply. as i writhed in discomfort she said to me --- "your ancestors have left something deep inside of you. but you're not ready." I was totally perplexed but knew i was preparing for The Something my ancestors had left there. I realize now that the hilot had pushed & pushed, said those words & helped activate it. IT was a seed.

As the years after that followed, I continued worked on newfilipina.com & participating in two discussions groups I had co-founded---Pagbabalikloob & Tagipusuon sg Babaylan. I wrote & created "Tagipusuon sg Babaylan" images & prose poetry at babaylan.com; chaired the FAWN2005 conference for Filipina leaders in New York City; created baybayinalive.com-- a site that shared & explored the deeper meanings of baybayin & other writing & symbols around the world; co-founded the international babaylan conferences & the Center of Babaylan Studies; created the Babaylan Mandala. At the center if this sacred mandala is the white tree I had been dreaming of for years. I named that tree the Bahala Na Tree. The branches of the tree are the baybayin shapes of HA & they curl gently in the air. The bottom of the BHLN tree's roots was BA & LA baybayin symbols to symbolize masculine & feminine energies come together, like a fertilized seed, so that the soul could be born & grow.

All of these works, & more, are from a deep place in my heart, Tagipusuon. Tagipusuon is the deep place of the heart where the soul/kaluluwa pulsates. Kaluluwa encompasses our whole body & soul, but it pulses energetically from the heart.

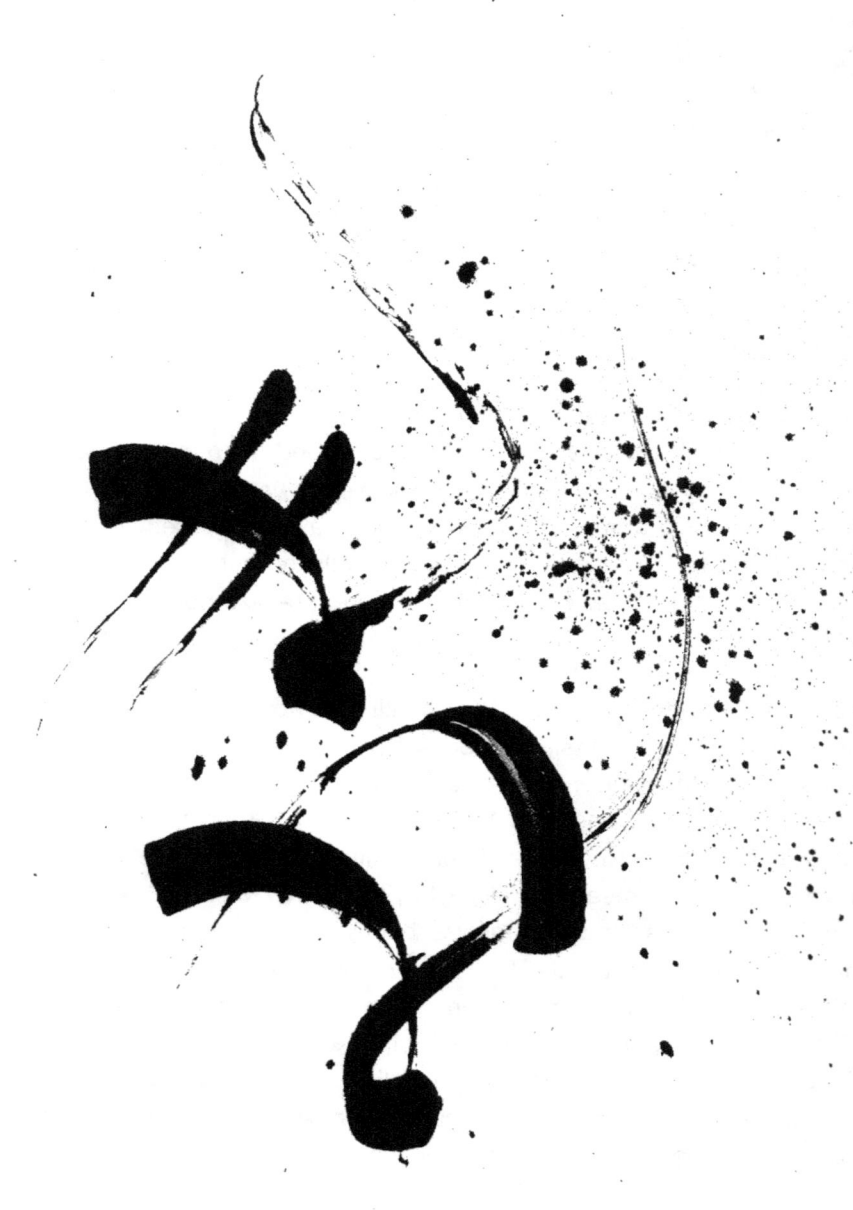

Ama - Father

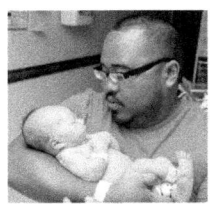

Bryan
Olathe, Kansas, USA

Since college, I had always wanted a tattoo, but wanted to make sure that it had true spiritual and personal meaning to me. When my dad unexpectedly passed a few months after I graduated college, I had a road map of what I wanted for a tattoo. It was devastating to my family, and I wanted to memorialize him somehow, but I got distracted with an MBA, my own career, and building my own family. A couple months after my wife and our son was born in 2012, I found an old notebook from my senior year of college that I had written some research in for the tattoo I wanted. In it, were some rough Baybayin translations that I had scribbled out, but never really got correctly translated. Now that my family is coming up on the tenth anniversary of my father's passing, and I am a father now, I got the idea to go through with getting a tattoo of Ama. It serves a double purpose of reminding me of my dad who was always making sure we knew about our Filipino heritage, to now being a father myself.

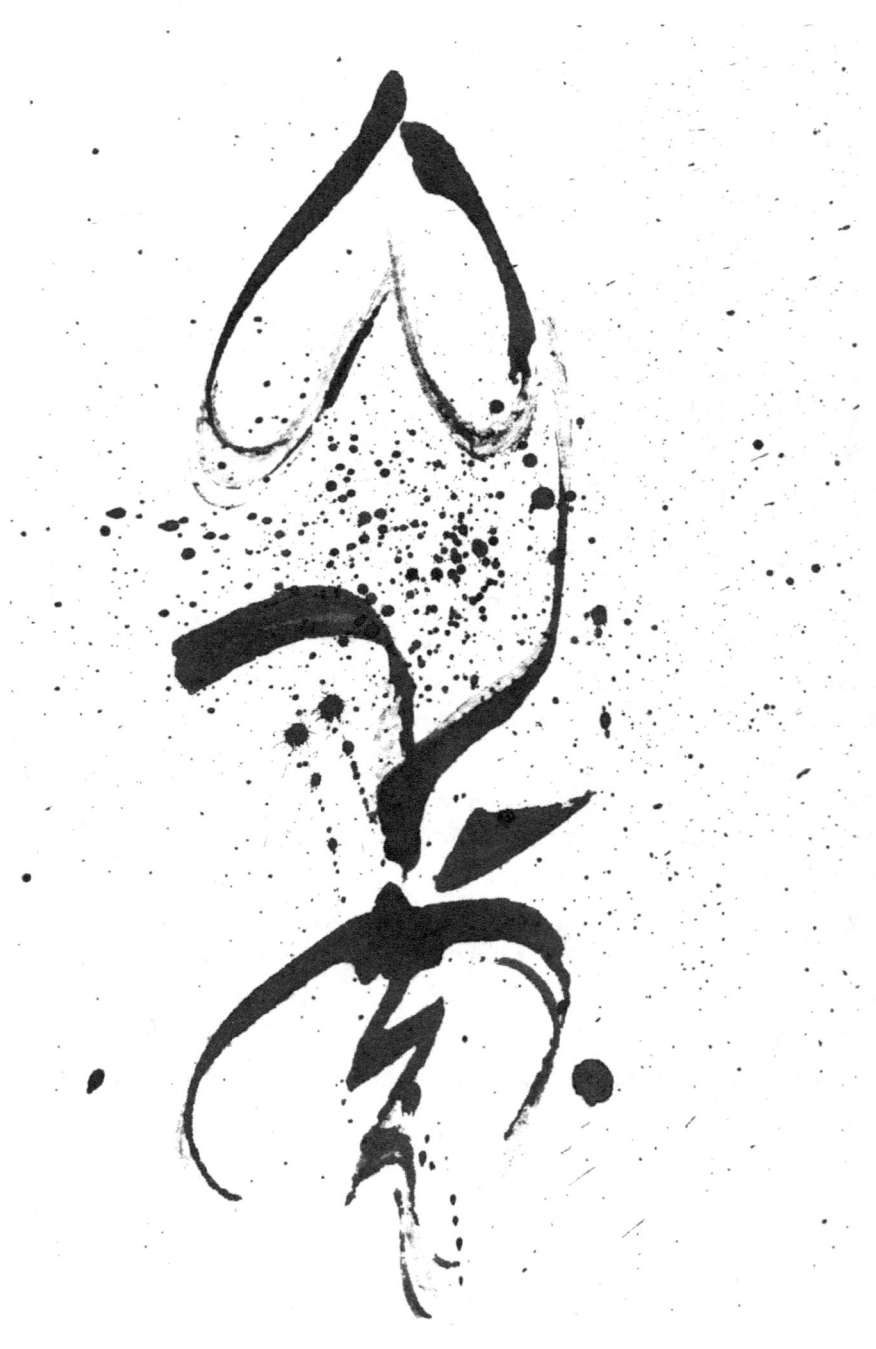

Bayani - Hero

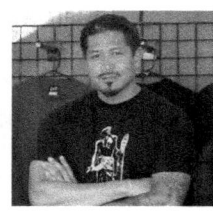

Joe
Oakland, California, Philippines
Bayaniart.com

Most people conceive the idea of a hero as a person who after their death has been recognized by a nation. The Oxford dictionary defines a hero as "a person, typically a man, who is admired or idealized for courage, outstanding achievements, or noble qualities" (Oxford Dictionary, 2007). It would be easier to define the word Bayani to the English translation of hero, but to the Filipino people, it has more elements. First, Bayani is not gender specific. Second, the definition of Bayani, in a Filipino traditional sense, is an unselfish act towards the human race; a person with extraordinary courage or bravery that ignores extreme danger and exhibits strength to overcome difficulties. Lastly, Bayani's never concern their own personal pleasure nor do they expect compensation for what they do, rather their actions are done out of kindness. In other words, a Bayani is one that humbly recognizes the interest of what is bigger that the individual, like the group, the community, the nation, humanity and the environment. The need to improve the state of humanity is instinctive and habitual.

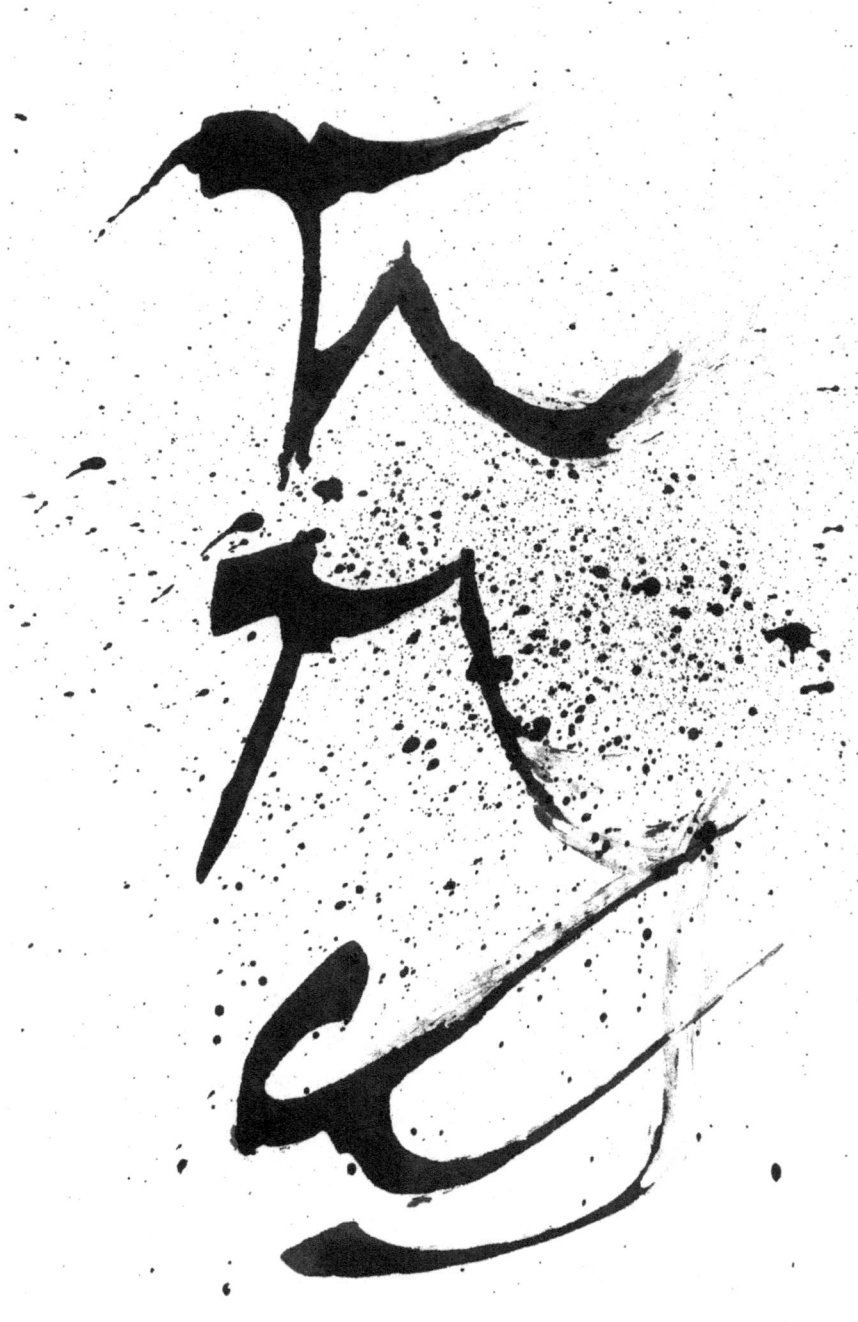

Dagat - Ocean

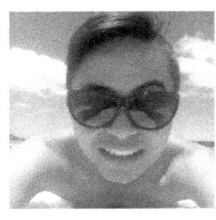

Jordan
Honolulu, Hawaii, USA

I chose the word "ocean" because the Pacific Ocean is my home, in a literal and symbolic sense. All life originated from the depths of the ocean. It's the ancestral home of all humanity. The ocean brought my family from the Philippines to Hawai'i. The Pacific Ocean connects me to my ancestral roots: it grounds me when I am lost, comforts me when I am sad, and rejuvenates me when I am tired. The ocean is my source of spiritual healing. The ocean is my home. The Ocean flows through my veins!

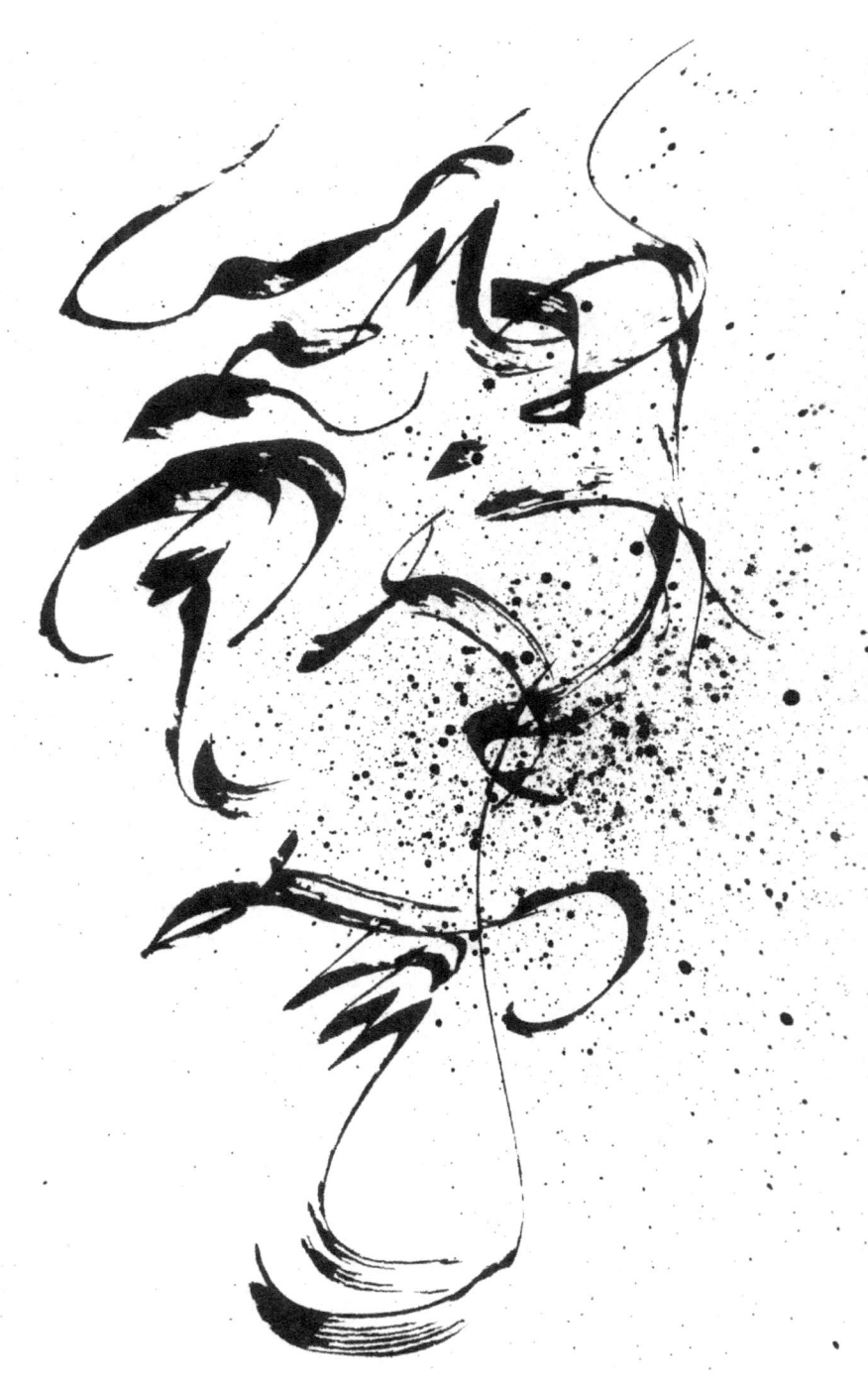

Emanuel

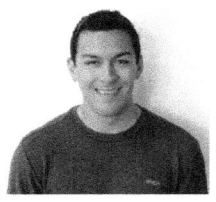

James
Walnut Creek, California, USA

Emanuel is the name of my sponsored child in Peru. On a mission trip to Lima, we worked with kids of the impoverished town of Manchay. Part of our trip was to visit a random family in the barrios. We visited Emanuel. Emanuel's smile and happiness even living in the poorest conditions immediately caught my heart. When I returned from Peru, I immediately set out to sponsor him. He wasn't in the database so I gave the center a picture I took with him and amazingly enough, they found him. After sponsoring him for a year, I returned to Peru, in the hopes of reuniting with him. After the 5th and last day, the center director brought him out and I was able to finally reunite with him. He embraced me with open arms and a big hug. I was hit with emotion as we had never met, and yet, he treated me like I was his long lost father. This is truly the highest moment I've had in my life. He immediately remembered me. He wouldn't leave my side the entire day. Sadly, 9 months after I returned, I found out that his living conditions got worse and he had to leave the care center and I lost him as a sponsor. When I was informed, I was heart-broken. However, just like the happiness and hope he showed living in those terrible conditions, I now have hope that he is ok. Ironically, Emanuel means "God with Us". Even though I'm not with him physically, he is in my heart forever. I will always cherish and remember him. I would love to have art done for this story as I would like to dedicate it to him.

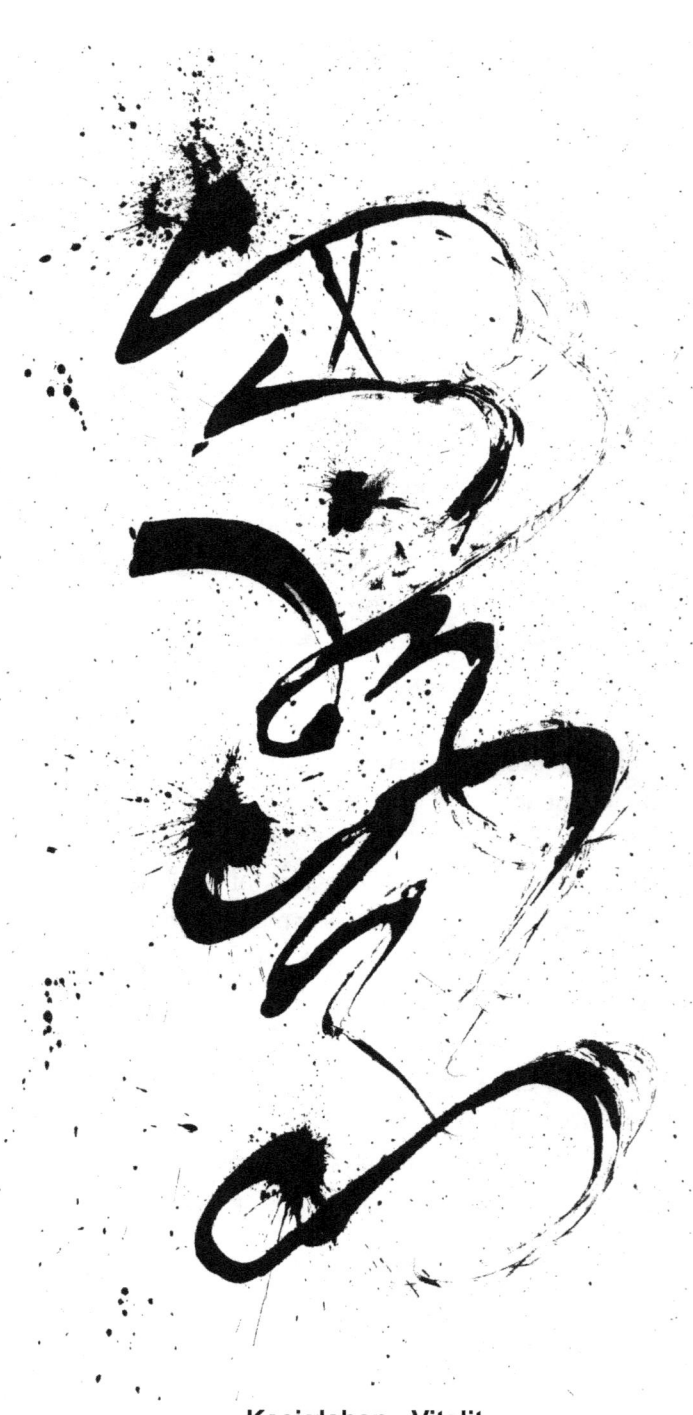

Kasiglahan - Vitality

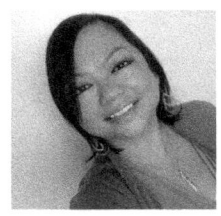

Michi
Honolulu, Hawaii, USA

I learned that Baybayin spelled Filipino words using the Filipino alphabet. My English name did not actually "translate" properly into Baybayin. Sets of symbols that represent ideas or words in Filipino?!? This thrilled me. After talking story and sharing a little about myself, I decided to have kasiglahan written on my pendant. I understood it to mean energy and spirituality, which were things I personally identified with throughout my life. I wore my pendant with pride during my college years. Little did I know how much fire and energy the pendant bearing this word would give me. This was one of the stepping stones to my activism in the Filipino community. It was lessons like these that opened my eyes to our rich Filipino heritage. This heritage was being lost with each passing generation. And I wanted to stop that from happening anymore. My activism ultimately leads me to Hawaii. I arrived here in 2005, marking the centennial or 100 years of Filipinos in America. I met all the historians, researchers and scholars I had only read about or heard about in one magnificent event filled year. Not only that, I was able to continue my work with the Filipino WWII veterans here in Hawaii. I currently work with the Filipino community in my professional career and help Filipino families plan for their future. I also have a personal commitment to my community through active participation in events that help preserve our culture like Fiesta and Filipino for Kids at the Filipino Community Center. One of the lessons I teach to our kids is about Baybayin and what the script means for us as Filipinos. One of the students asked, "Why did we lose Baybayin?" And I replied, "It's not lost because you're learning it today. " I only hope they find the same inspiration that I found when I first learned Baybayin all those years ago in the booth at Pistahan. Kasiglahan, the word that I thought meant energy and spirituality also carried another meaning that I truly believe has given me the drive to work for the community. That meaning is zeal, which means enthusiasm, passion, fervor and eagerness... all the things I feel when I serve my Filipino community. It was only the beginning when I found the Filipino word in Baybayin that represented me all those years ago.

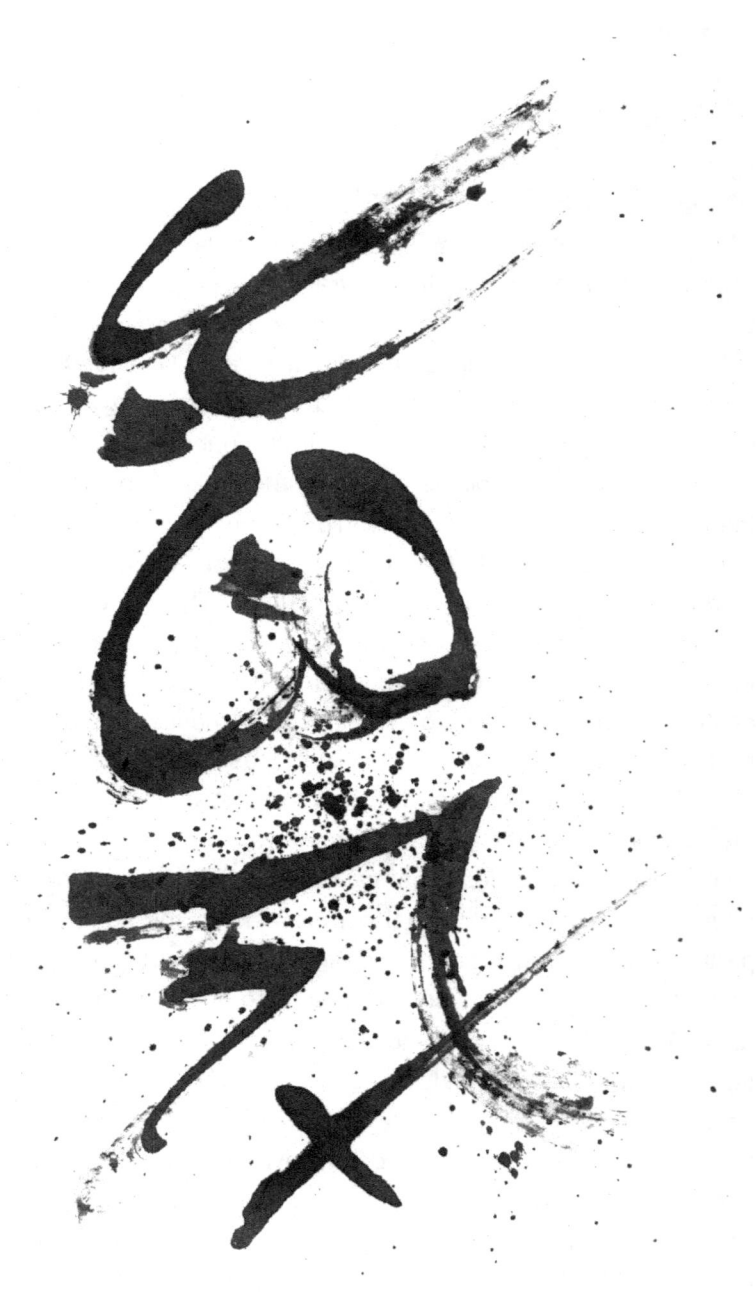

Tubig - Water

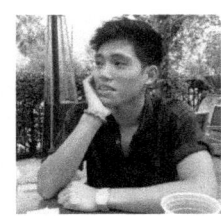

Andrew
Houston, Texas, USA

What separates me from the Philippines is the ocean. I live in Texas, which is the complete opposite of home. I miss my home everyday and I long to be home again. Recently, when I found out about baybayin, I began doing research about Filipino history. I've noticed how we as a people have time and time again praised nature and the ocean in our culture and language. Looking at our history, we are navigators of the ocean and it is only natural that we adapt and move. Therefore, I cannot blame my parents from moving me from the islands to the US. We moved because of the financial and prosperous benefits of the US. Filipinos long for prosperity because of the struggles in our home country. Hence, Filipino Americans are raised to get an education and become a successful professional because we know the price we pay to move from our home to a new home. Not only do we prosper and succeed in this new country, but we adapt so well that we adopt other cultures. Which brings me to the common Filipino American identity dilemma. One of our greatest strengths as a people also hinders us from unity. But thanks to nationalist movements like baybayin, we as a people can keep our cultural identity and move along the river of change. It's like the old Chinese proverb of having a "mind or heart like water." We are Filipinos who are not afraid of change because it is in our blood to travel the seas and live a long prosperous life. Mabuhay and travel well through the waters to all my Filipinos.

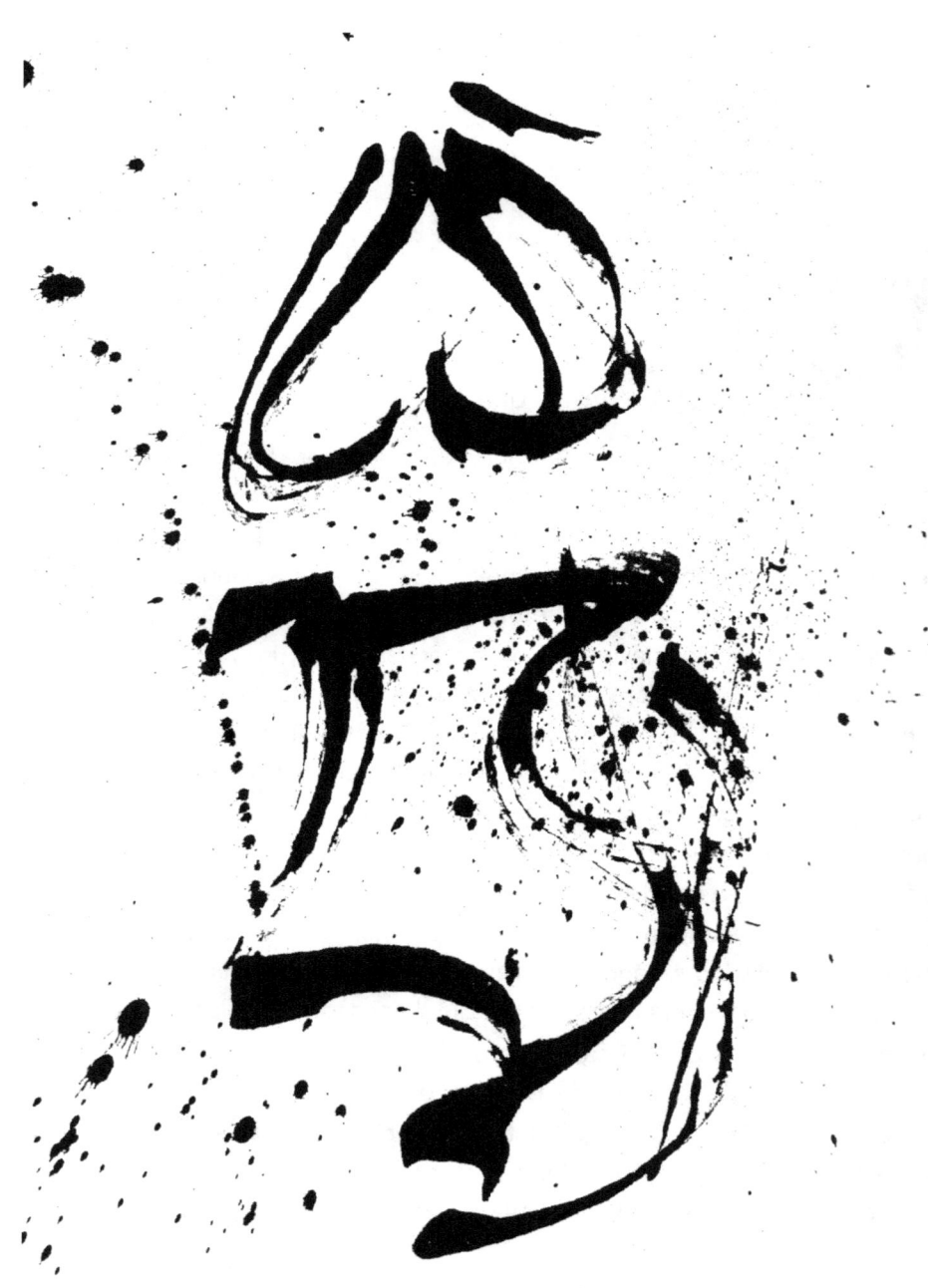

Bigay - Give

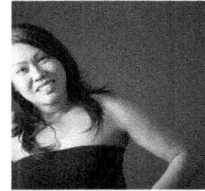

Genevieve
Daly City, California, USA
Soulciety.org

Giving is a strong and consistent part of my upbringing and has helped mold me and my family to who and what we are today.

As long as I can remember, giving is what my parents have always done. Sacrifice also comes with giving. My father immigrated to the US in 1975, leaving my mother and two older brothers behind. All he knew here in America were his Philippine University batch mates who later became our family network.

Tatay, as I call my father, sacrificed his comfort to give his family better opportunities. Since the moment he set foot here, giving is all he and my mother did. Nanay and my two brothers reunited with Tatay a year later. Nanay then worked graveyard doing blue collar work. Even though she was University-educated, blue collar work is all she could find because she couldn't speak English well. Financially, my mother didn't have to work, but she dedicated all of her pay sending money back to the Philippines and putting Tatay's seven brothers and sisters, her two nieces, and many more through college, on top of raising five children.

They never turned their cheek to those who were in need even if it meant lugging their five children around to help at a church or alumni association event. I spent a lot of time wrapping lumpia or serving punch for these events.

Even if it meant lending their last dollar, my parents didn't want people to struggle knowing that they could have done something to help. This kind of upbringing has influenced my work ethic and passion for community advocacy because despite what I go through and what I encounter, it will never, NEVER compare to what my parents had to go through to make it for themselves, their children, and their family. So, if you have the opportunity to give, even if it's your last penny or even if it's to spare a minute to help someone who is struggling, then you should, because you have the ability to.

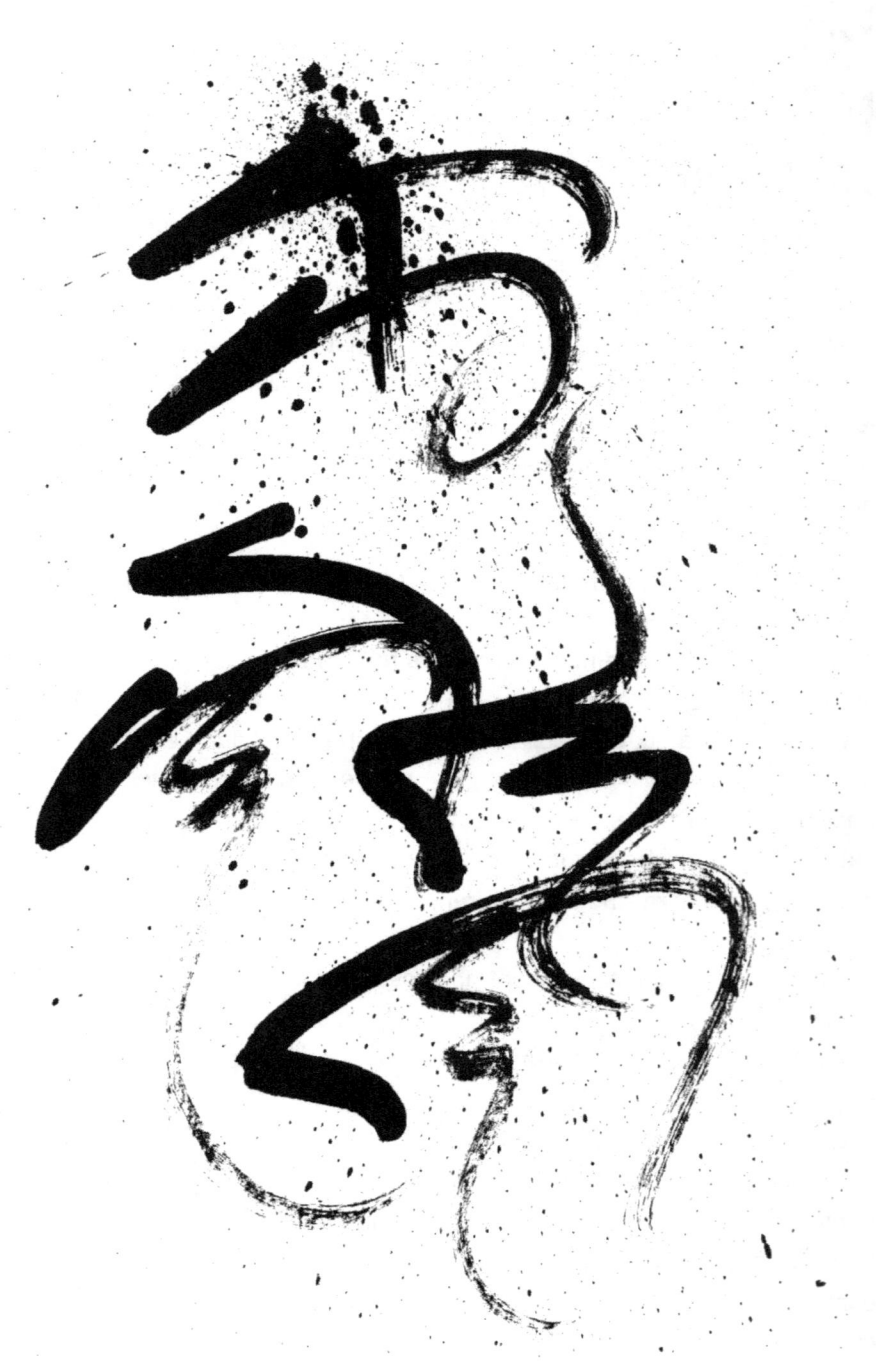

Kasalanan - Sin

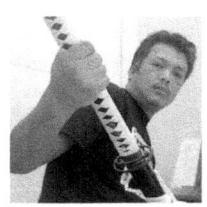

Norman
Indio, California, USA
Baybayinfonts.com

Along with knowledge & understanding, the life-lessons we gain from our experiences shape who we are as a person.

I am not your average Catholic Filipino. I am an atheist. The experiences we, rare Filipino atheists, encountered that set us to the path of universal enlightenment may be worth noting, or it may be worth nothing, or both. So just let me tell you mine anyway. It starts as, "like many other young Filipinos, I went to Catholic school…"

A priest attempted to molest me when I was in 5th. Grade. Wait… that was awful. I'd rather not speak of that. However, please note, that encounter didn't f*&! me up (literally & figuratively). No. That was just one of the many complex reasons that made me question organized religion. I actually had a long time to think & research theology. But that took decades and it's long & boring. So, I digress, here's one with a bit more of an anecdotal feel:

When I was a young lad, I enjoyed courting other guys' girlfriend behind their backs. I was quite successful at the game. I liked the conquest and satisfaction I get from knowing that I can get a girl to like me more than their more popular & good looking jock of a boyfriend. See, I was our high school's odd, nerdy, dark, and artistic kid.

One year, we had a young & pretty postulant (nun-in-training) substitute for our teacher. She was only three and a half years older than my peers and I. Being young and bold, I befriended her asked her out to a couple of "friendly" dates. And with a little bit of coaxing from my part and some reluctance in her part, she entertained my advances, the more "reasonable" and less "improper" ones at least. However, in the end, she turned me down gently, stating our age difference and the fact that she (in her words) "was engaged to Jesus Christ our Lord" and nothing or nobody can change that.

It was a big kick to the ego, the one that I precariously built up through the years from the string of stolen conquests & romances. There I was, the king of the thieves of hearts, rejected. The only guy I couldn't steal a girl from was the Son of God himself! It dawned on me in the end that, if I can't beat a long dead messiah, I might as well throw down the towel and sing: "I wish that I have Jesus' girl… where can I find a young nun like that? Jesus' girl!"

But not all my "sins" end with such a finality as atheism. Some of my guilt and regrets move me to make up for my past disservices. Some lead me to create numerous computer typefaces/fonts Baybayin and Surat Mangyan. And some lead me to writing and teaching about the value of our past, our culture, our heritage, and our legacy.

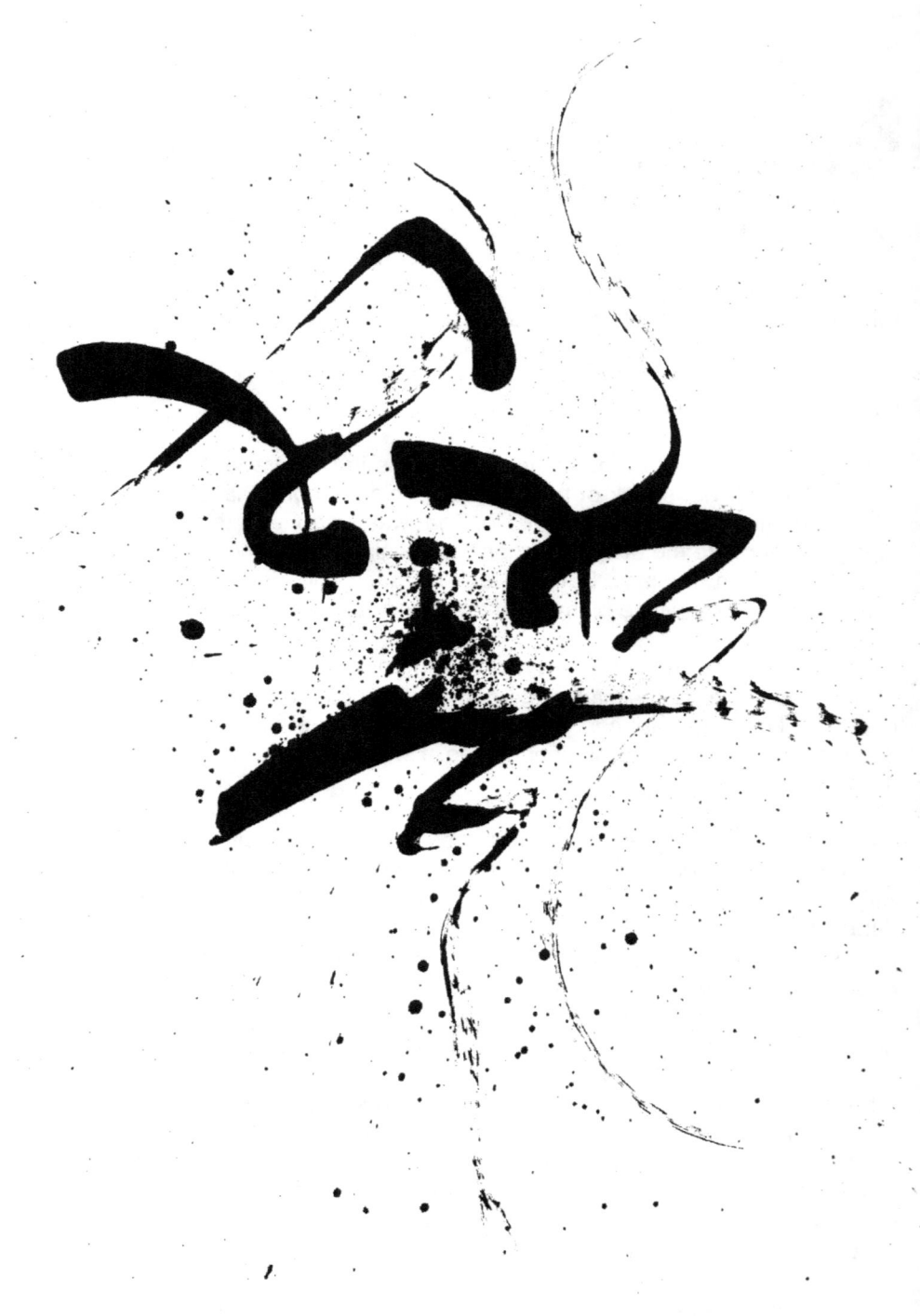

Masigasig - Effervescent

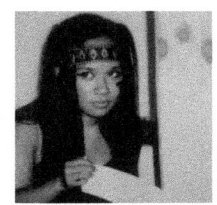

Felma
London, UK

'Effervescent a word bubbling beneath the surface'

To me the word Effervescent means celebration, joyfulness, awakening of emotions and enthusiasm for life and art. It has been a long journey to feel worthy of this word, although I never thought I would deserve to own this word, especially to describe my visual artist persona and unconscious self. Consequently, the word effervescent has always been bubbling beneath the surface from my childhood to present.

As an only child creating art was my first experience of feeling full of blissful contentment, an escapism allowing me to lose myself in a world of fairytales, angels and super hero's. Art gave me the confidence to strive in a predominantly white catholic school in the 80's and finding my voice as an effervescent artist. I was bullied for being the only British Filipino in the class, and the children back then thought I was Chinese. I was also quiet as a child, although during art projects at school, my art started to get recognition and fellow students and teachers praised me for my natural artistic abilities. I was no longer distinguished by my racial identity, which gave me an incentive to develop my artistic skills, by practicing daily with the use of various art materials creating images from my imagination and general media.

My passion for creating art grew throughout secondary school, college and university days. After my Bachelor's degree in Fine Art, I was encouraged by my tutors to participate in solo/ group art exhibitions. In particular, on weaving and developing my artist persona, I came across this group called 'London Biennale art group' founded and directed by avant-garde, Filipino/ International artist David Medalla. Being part of the London Biennale group gave me a platform to network, exhibit with other like minded artists and supported me to express myself through producing unconventional mix-media artwork(s) and performance art. This gave me the confidence to exhibit my artwork to the general public for the first time and express my effervescent artist persona.

Currently, I am still a practicing 'effervescent' artist (based in London, UK) and embarking on my final year of my Master's degree training as an Art Psychotherapist. The Effervescent Art Psychotherapist side of me represents my unconscious-self, compassionate and true-ego (soul/spirit). My desire to become an Art Psychotherapist springs from two passions in my life, admiring/ creating art and my wish to help vulnerable people discover their own effervescent voices through Art Psychotherapy.

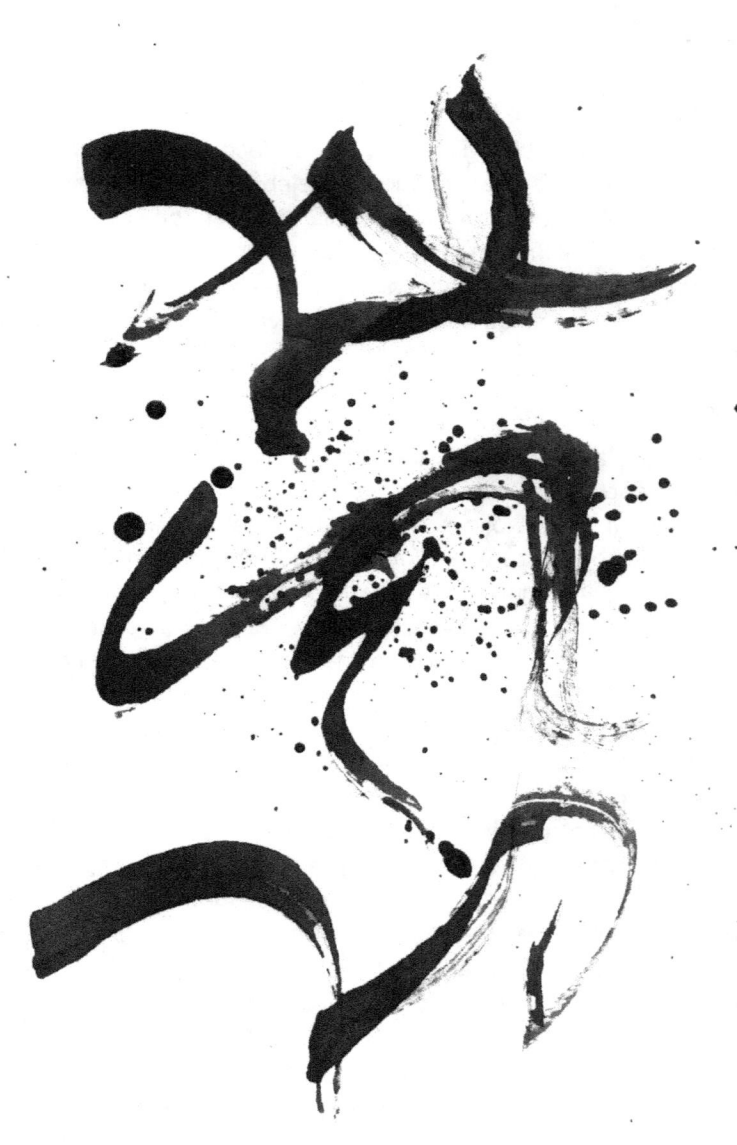

Malaya - Free

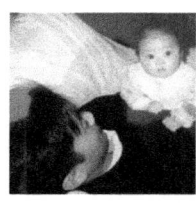

Michael
Berekley, California, USA
Mikemojica.com

I was born in the Philippines and came to the U.S. when I was two years old. I grew up bilingual until I hit Kindergarten. I had memories of speaking Tagalog to my family and especially loved speaking to my Uncle Dennis. For some reason I grew up only knowing English. To this day I can't understand nor speak Filipino or Tagalog. My mom had spoken to my ex-wife about my upbringing and it was then that I found out why I no longer knew how to speak Tagalog. My mom expressed guilt over listening to what my kindergarten teachers had told her.

When I was young, I would speak Tagalog to my teachers and they told my parents to only speak English to me at home. I wasn't angry at my mom. I understood that they were just trying to help me fit in. I was angry with the system and lack of culture that the U.S. education system exhibits. The stories I had learned in history, only to know more truths of about how this country was actually built. The land stolen from the natives.

When my daughter was born I wanted to give her a name that was feminine and also identified her as Filipino. While brainstorming with my-ex wife down the freeway, the name Malaya came up. Since I didn't know Tagalog, it wasn't until she was born that someone told me that it meant to be free, "Freedom". To this day I encourage her to express herself and to speak up even when it goes against what I want. I want her to have a powerful voice and to not be afraid of telling people who she is. She's a teenager now and sometimes it is uncomfortable to have conversations with her where we disagree and where I'm not consciously abusing my power to change her mind. I would not have it any other way.

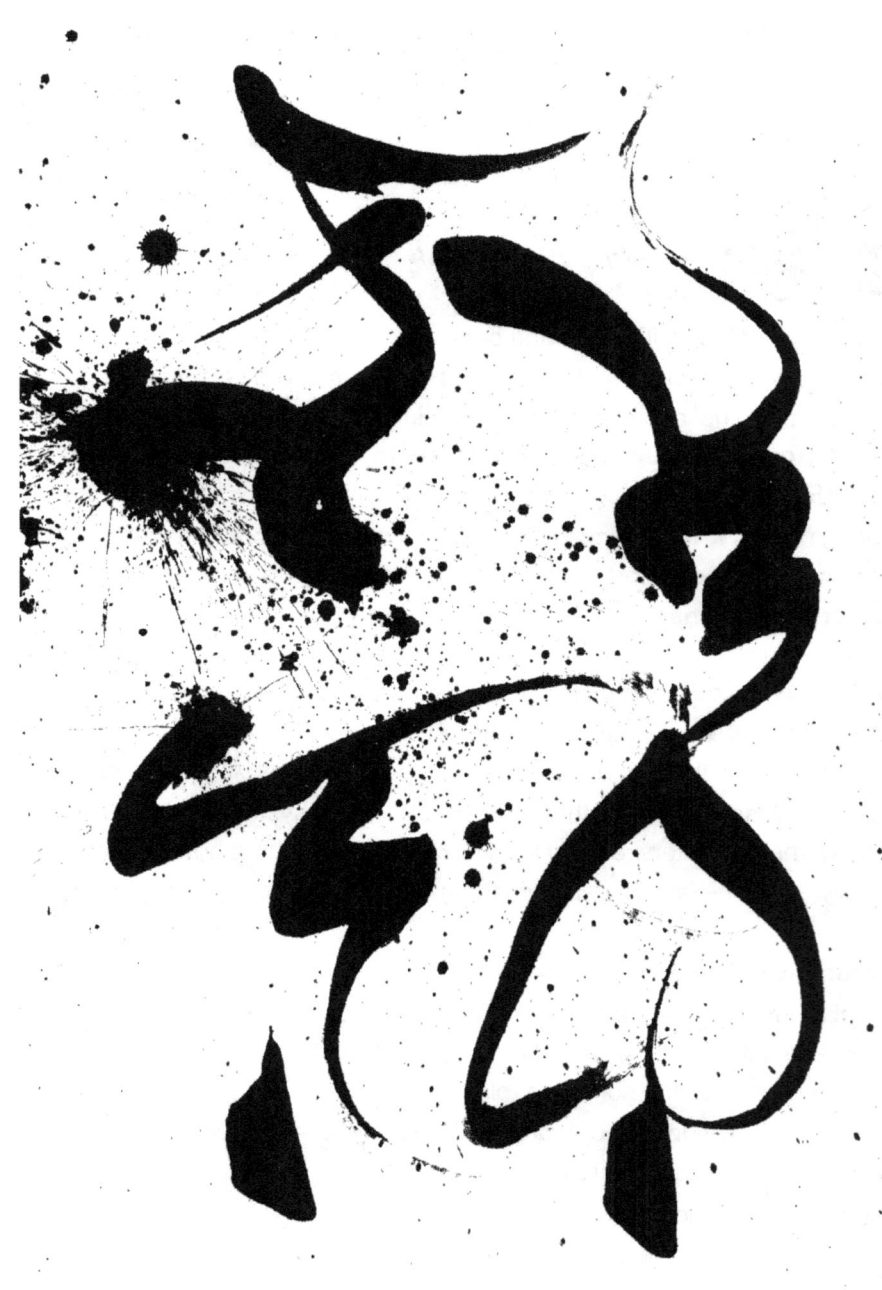

Pasalubong - Gift

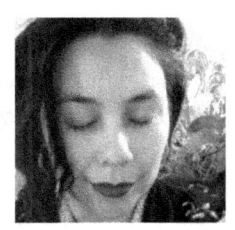

Iraya
San Francisco, California, USA

My name is a gift. Fate, luck, cultural recovery, root seekings = a Gift. Being outsider or unclaimed= Gift. Always being not what anyone would expect=Gift. This life, such a Gift. Pinay=Gift. My Mixed Blood = Gift.

I knew it was a volcano on a map, they found their baby on a map....

Pasalubong: "A gift I give you for welcoming me back."

I am a visitation. I thank you. I know I remind you of what has happened to our peeps, or what could come next. Thank you for having me here. A gift.

Named for a tribe, a place, a language never learned...one of the only Filipino things I carried, a name I pronounced, a name I defended, it always felt so sacred to me. And now a deeper understanding of why.

I feel my many places I come from, my many cultures visible and invisible are some of this gift.

A-named-for-a-volcano-baby, a Third World Liberation baby born in SF, came out light-skinned but half-brown so Filipino-brown, half-olive Baby. Filipino-American born Fillmore ghetto man I-Hotel one-of-ten-roast-a-pig-in the– ground-south-of-marketworking poor/class-villager-ethnic studies student-strike-PACE-Father. Italiana warbabyred-diaper-partisan-landed excelsior-avenues-artisti-metaphysical peasant/jewish/sardinian mixed-class Mother....Imperfect union made a baby, an experimental baby like me. Illness. Separation. When Filipino dad went away, Filipino mystery all day. Solved the Mystery. Began to know-ing. Forgave again...

Traced my roots and connected with those who would claim me...Blood and otherwise chosen. Made in Cali, born on Geary Boulevard. Trying to understand who-she-isstill-everyday-a-baby, the everydayness of it all. Confused but clear Baby.

Put me in a baby- beauty -contest-and-had-to-split-the-prize-with-a-white-baby-Baby. Mixed babies couldn't fully receive trophies in the 70's. We naturally got half, if anything. Not Like I Believe in It anyway, but still.

Filipina-America but Mestiza -Mixed-Clement Street, a half-Italiana Richmond & Sunset District childhood, Grandparents, Geary blvd, friends in neighborhood of mostly Chinese & Japanese & Korean & Cambodian, a couple Black kids, Latins, Mixed kids, Whites, one Russian ...not many Filipinos...and cousins I didn't yet know. One Filipina big sis in elementary schoolyard, she gave me Ate energy in her Derby jackets, Ben Davis pants and Chinese embroidered Mary Janes, and saw me when no one else did, thank you for living down the street and giving me Pinayism. Gifts.

I'm an IT'S IT. I am year of the Dog-Doggie Diner. I am overcast.

Sorsogon and Lucca, Mountain people on all sides.

Father's fam gave me Blood knowedge: Grandma Marquita, Filipinos in the Fillmore, Seattle, Hawaii, Poetry Uncles and cousins, Diva Aunties and lumpias...stories of razorblades in the updos, gangs, Manilatown, Grandparents, teenage marriages, from the same village, merchant marines, Working Class herstories/histories, self-taught artists, dancers, weavers, Asiana-American Avant Garde ,Uncle Ray "Filipino Two-Spirit", Discos, Polk Street, Watsonville, Zen, gas station attendants, janitors, farmworkers, Alaska, boxers, maids, healers, bouncers, hotel workers, The Tenderloin, martial arts, "Bruce Lee", drag show waitresses, numbers runners, community organizers, absences, reputations, prayers, "a whole caboose full of uncles", unknown tribes, outer-married, countless Mestizas/os cousins, "mini united-nations", Style, Ritual, J-town, poolhalls, legends, confusion, Kearny Street, "We won't move!", Provinces, The Aves, Chinatown, Jazz again & again, "I Remember You", loss, solace, Agung, siblings, who becomes the Manang/Manong, Ifugao dreams...

Walking herself to church everyday, losing Grandma 100 years later after the war, in 1998, receiving her spirit.

All Gifts I will never be confused on again. Forgiveness learned at an early age. Thanking ancestors.

I found some Filipina girlhood for me, finding more of it every year.,...filling the longing. And again now in my early 40's: birthdays of noodles & rice & ravioli & halo halo & cheese & bread & lumpia & salads with bee pollen & fish with coconut & longbeans & vegan bbq & ube birthday ice cream and whatever else.....

Wondering about Balikbayan boxes as an adult, no one to send them to or receive them from. No one to hear from or to write to. No long distance on that side. Searching. I keep several boxes at home now.

Gifts.

Visiting Grandma Marquita in the TL, learning how to prepare milkfish, Altars, astral projections, prayers, deeper wisdoms, healings, wondering how she knew. Calling her Grandma not Lola, our whole family did. Even though I didn't grow up to learn Pilipino language, each year my roots call me more and more. She always welcomed her stray grandchildren, separated by drama and rejection and fate. Her Embrace stays with me.

Tropical space sisterhoods, Futura Pinayisms. So now I become Ate to some very Special Ones...Still Honoring all the 90's chosen sisters & siblings, QTPOC punk rock friends, Mestiza Sacto runaway girls raising themselves in a shitty car all the way to Gliman St. An artist/organizer/badass survivor from Oakland/Pangasinan /Houston. Queer 'N Asian, APS & APLBN, JADED, wherehouse gigs. Radical dykes, women's symbols, zines. Throwing/shaking things off on the dancefloor. "Are you Pinay?", conference crashing, CCSF, Club Red, Junk, my old band Sta-Prest, Queerpunk, RG, Woman of Color ClubLife, "Pounding Rhythms", working the door. Coco Club, Epicenter, Brown Suga, Mimi, Trinity, Mail Order Brides, mentors, beats, noise, thrift stores, stickers, marches, Hapa everything, putting on shows, fresh fruit at the End-up, getting schooled on House...coming out again as Femme...Gigi bringing the (a)eromestizaness to us all. Me always outside/inside, content with being unplaceable., nursing my 5 different hair textures, caregiving, living, hospice, passings. Honorings.

Seeking and learning traditions of my Elders, seen and unseen. Being unafraid to speak on grief as well as beauty...Thank you past/present/future for all these life-giving forces.

A Gift.

The Author

Kristian Kabuay was born in the Philippines and raised in the San Francisco Bay Area. He spent his college years in the Philippines where he honed his knowledge about the native ancient writing system, Baybayin. Kristian is a self-taught artist influenced by calligraphy, graffiti, abstract art, indigenous culture, technology and Asian writing systems.

As a leading authority for the propagation and instruction of the Philippine script, he developed a modern performance style of the writing system called Tulang Kalis (Poetry of the Sword) and introduced it as Filipino Calligraphy with a series of live demonstrations and lectures at the Asian Art Museum in October 2012. He has spoken at numerous schools and institutions around the world such as Stanford University, UC Berkeley, SF State University, UC Davis, Sonoma State, University of the Philippines and the National Anthropology Museum of Madrid.

Currently based in San Francisco, Kristian has been tirelessly advocating a reawakening of the indigenous spirit through decolonization and Baybayin. Conscious about the role he plays, Kristian launched his own company around the script specializing custom art, translations, books and apparel. This lead to collaborations with t-shirt, hat and skateboard companies. Kristian just completed a European tour of Paris, Madrid, London and Brussels in July, 2013 and is currently working on a documentary.